the book of sacramental basics

tad guzie

paulist press   *new york/mahwah*

Calligraphy by Noreen Guzie
Cover Design by Tim McKeen

Library of Congress
Catalog Card Number: 81-83189

ISBN: 0-8091-2411-4

Published by Paulist Press
997 Macarthur Boulevard
Mahwah, NJ 07430

Printed and bound in the
United States of America

contents

introduction 1

1 the rhythm that makes life human 5

2 asking the right question 24

3 from symbol to sacrament 38

4 a workable definition 52

5 the sacramental process 71

6 sacraments for children 92

7 befriending our symbols 117

notes 136

suggested readings 139

introduction

*B*ringing together the old and the new is the task of the church in every age. Jesus said as much when he praised the scribe, the guardian of tradition in his own day, who had become a disciple of the kingdom of heaven. Such a person is like a householder who brings out of his storeroom things both old and new (Mt 13:52).

The renewal flowing from Vatican II has brought forth many new things, new ways of understanding and celebrating our ancient faith. But it takes time for the new and the old to come together comfortably. For a good while we seem to stand with one foot planted in each camp. This seems to describe where we stand with the sacraments, as we move into the last quarter of the twentieth century. All of our rites have been rewritten, but we bring to them a mixture of attitudes flowing from two different schools of thought.

The old school emphasizes the grace that a sacrament brings to the individual soul and the right disposition each person needs in order to receive that grace. The new school stresses celebrating rather than receiving, the assembly which celebrates, and the lived faith experience which is being celebrated.

The old school tends to see the initiative of God toward ourselves as linked with the church's sacramental system so intimately that grace is liable not to happen for a person unless a sacrament is received. The new school sees the initiative of God toward us as a grace that is already present in the world, through the fact of Jesus Christ. This grace, this love of God, is celebrated in the sacraments, but it is not first contacted in the sacraments.

One view holds that we are all sinners, and we come to the celebration of a sacrament in order to receive something we do not possess, namely the grace of God. The other view insists that if we are all sinners, we are also *graced* sinners. We are never in the position of *not* being loved by God. We come together to celebrate that love, not to get something which is absent to us. We come together to savor that love, to remember its presence, and to go away from the sacrament with a deeper appropriation of the love that surrounds us with every breath we take.

The old school places great weight on the presence of the Lord at the moment of the sacramental celebration. The new school wants to emphasize that the problem is not the Lord's presence to us, but rather our presence to him. This is what any sacramental celebration tries to overcome—not God's distance from us, because there is none, but rather our distance from God and our unawareness of the love that is there for us.

This book is an effort to bring together the old and the new. It is not just a matter of harmonizing differences, because not everything can be harmonized. There have been blind spots in our past tradition; these have to be taken into account along with the insights and contributions of the past. There are also many new questions which the past did not ask, and which we have only begun to explore. Still, for all the gaps there may be in our knowledge of the mysteries which we celebrate in sacrament, I will stand by the rather bold title I have chosen for this book. I leave it to my reader to judge at the end whether the book has truly covered "the basics," old and new.

The book does not give a separate treatment of each sacrament. It deals with the meaning of celebrating sacramentally, and so each ritual comes up for discussion in many different contexts. For specific treatments of eucharist and penance, I refer the reader to other books of mine: *Jesus and the Eucharist* (Paulist, 1974), and *The Forgiveness of Sin* (Thomas More, 1979). Some of the ideas in the pages that follow have appeared in various articles I have written, especially for *U.S. Catholic,* and in cassettes recorded for *The National Catholic Reporter.*

This book is dedicated to all the people whom I have had the privilege of meeting in courses and workshops around the United States and Canada, and who have kept me asking the important questions. It is dedicated also to my wife Noreen, whose suggestions have been even finer than the calligraphy she has done for the book.

University of Calgary
Epiphany, 1981

the rhythm that makes life human

chapter one

*I*t all began with an experience. A group of people had their lives turned around by a carpenter's son. Many centuries later an English poet would put these words on that experience:

> Let him easter in us, be a dayspring to the dimness of us,
>   be a crimson-cresseted east,
> More brightening her, rare-dear Britain, as his reign rolls,
>   Pride, rose, prince, hero of us, high-priest,
> Our hearts' charity's hearth's fire, our thoughts'
>   chivalry's throng's Lord.

The first followers of the man from Nazareth had still other titles for him: son of man, savior, messiah, the anointed one, the Christ. They had their own words for telling their story, and their many stories were finally pulled together into the book we call the New Testament. Paul tells his story in a different way from Matthew, and Luke shapes his version differently from John. But despite the variations, the first followers always seemed to tell their story with the same excitement and sense of exaltation, even breathlessness, conveyed by those lines from Gerard Manley Hopkins.[1]

5

So much was Jesus a man of God that his followers came to call him by the godly name of "Lord," that climactic and ringing word at the end of Hopkins' poem. In their easter experience, they recognized him as a man so fully *from* God and so fully *for* God that the followers of Jesus had to change their ideas about God. God had now shown his face in the person of Jesus, and shown it so vividly that all their notions of God had to be widened to include their experience of Jesus.

Eventually dogmas would develop, hammered out through the course of many centuries and many arguments about how best to express Jesus' relationship to the Father. But in the beginning, Jesus' followers were not preoccupied with ideas *about* him. They mainly wanted to tell the story of their experience *of* him. And this was always a story of how Jesus eastered in them, how he was a dayspring to their dimness.

When something exciting happens, it is the human thing to celebrate that happening. To do so, we spontaneously turn to what is familiar. Old rituals take on new meanings when an intensely lived experience is brought to them. A ritual like a family dinner somehow becomes something new and larger when it celebrates new life, a birth, a rebirth, a reconciliation.

So it was for the first followers of Jesus. Water baptism was one ritual already at hand, well known to the first-century world. The followers of Jesus quickly adopted it to express their entrance into the mystery of Jesus and their whole sense of a new beginning, of a new Spirit let loose in their midst.

We tell our stories not just in words and narratives, but even more basically in signs and actions, "charged" actions like a warm embrace, or giving someone a gift, or sharing a meal. In just this way, baptism was a most basic way in which the disciples of Jesus told their story. It was a story of how when they went into the water, they went into the tomb with Jesus and joined him in death, in order to be raised with him and live a new life

(Rom 6). What more "basic" way could there be of telling the "basic" story?

There was another ritual at hand, known to a number of Jewish groups in Jesus' time. We read of it in documents left behind by some of the monastic communities who lived in the deserts of Palestine. It was a meal of bread and wine which looked forward to the coming of the Messiah and to the feast that would be held on that great day. On the eve of his death, Jesus give this ritual a new significance. He charged it with the meaning of his own life and ministry and death, his sharing and breaking and outpouring of himself. So we are not surprised to read that his followers, right from the beginning, met in one another's homes for the "breaking of the bread" (Acts 2).

This was another form of telling their story. They had other rituals, other gatherings for prayer. But breaking the bread and sharing the cup were a unique way of remembering Jesus. Not remembering things *about* him, as though they were nostalgically recalling the past. What they remembered around the table was that the great Day of the Lord is today, and the Lord Jesus was then and there eastering in them.

What we observe here is a very normal and profoundly human dynamic: An important experience is retold in story and remembered in festivity. The retelling and remembering in turn help us to re-enter everyday lived experience with a sense of refreshment and a new sense of purpose.

The same kind of thing happens at family celebrations—birthdays, anniversaries, reunions. Famous family stories are retold: Remember the time when Uncle George's teeth fell into the soup? The same games are played: Let's play charades, the way we did last year. The same songs are sung: Happy birthday—Happy anniversary—And play the one that Grandma always likes. The cake is cut and shared, on the same best dishes, with the same best candlesticks on the table.

One Christmas was so much like another. . . . I can never
remember whether it snowed for six days and six nights when I
was twelve, or whether it snowed for twelve days and twelve
nights when I was six. . . . For dinner we had turkey and blazing
pudding, and after dinner the Uncles sat in front of the fire,
loosened all buttons, put their large moist hands over their watch
chains, groaned a little and slept. Mothers, aunts and sisters
scuttled to and fro, bearing tureens. . . . And then, at tea the
recovered Uncles would be jolly; and the ice cake loomed in the
centre of the table like a marble grave. Auntie Hannah laced her
tea with rum, because it was only once a year.

Bring out the tall tales now that we told by the fire as the
gaslight bubbled like a diver. . . . Always on Christmas night there
was music. An uncle played the fiddle. Auntie Hannah, who had
got on to the parsnip wine, sang a song about Bleeding Hearts
and Death, and then another in which she said her heart was like
a Bird's Nest; and then everybody laughed again.[2]

No one ever leaves such celebrations without a renewed awareness of who we are, for good or for ill, as a family. Festivity picks
us off our feet and returns us to everyday life with new eyes.

Let us look more closely at each of the elements in the cycle. Note, first of all, that there is a difference between *lived* experience and what we might call *raw* experience.

At the end of each working day I leave my office, lock the
door, take the elevator down to the main floor, walk to the park-
ing lot, get into the car, drive out and turn left onto Crowchild,
and make my way home. This is a raw experience, and nothing
has ever happened to make me raise these activities to the level
of *lived* experience. Things would be different if, day after day, I
had to wait in a long queue of cars so that it took me five or ten
minutes, day after day, before I could make that left turn, with
still more waiting in traffic jams all the rest of the way home.

A raw experience starts to become lived experience when
significance comes into play—an awareness that the experience
does touch the quality of my life. In the example I just gave, the

raw activities of closing shop and making my way home are in themselves quite unrelated to the meaning of my life, quite "insignificant." It takes something like daily frustration, which *is* significant, to get me to raise this everyday routine to the level of lived experience. At that level I would have to recognize the frustration, reflect on it, see what it does to my life, and deal with it. Perhaps I would have to look for another kind of transportation, or even find a home in a more convenient location. But as things stand in my case, getting home from work is not frustrating, not significant, and therefore does not invite reflection. Many of our daily routines are like this: Brushing one's teeth or tying one's shoes in the morning rarely needs to become a profoundly lived experience.

Lived experience therefore involves recognizing significance in the raw experiences of life. But something more is also needed. The significance has to be related in some way to myself. A neighbor is robbed; a friend falls ill with cancer; a relative loses a job. These events are immediately and objectively significant, but they might not immediately impinge upon my life. Perhaps such events should remind me of my own vulnerability, or draw my attention to things in my own life that I ought to appreciate more. If this is to happen, reflection is needed. In its most basic form, reflection is simply the act of *relating* a raw experience to the meaning of one's own life.

There are joys and sorrows, good fortunes and bad, that we often forget or lay aside or even try to repress. Conflict and disagreement, for example, are among the normal stuff of any human relationship. But friendships and marriages break down when these raw experiences are not reflected upon, acknowledged, and assimilated into the relationship. The process called "healing" often has to do with finally appropriating raw experiences that have been repressed or laid aside for too long.

Even what appear to be happy times are not automatically *lived* experiences. Sometimes years go by before we appreciate and fully own the significance of a joyful moment shared with a friend. And sometimes what appear to be happy times later turn out to have been superficial and insignificant.

One of the great misfortunes of the question-and-answer method of the old catechisms was that people's real experiences were ignored. Not denied—merely discounted. The right answer was what mattered. It did not matter that one had not yet experienced the question. Even more important, the questions coming out of people's lived experience were generally not the questions which the catechism answered.

This is probably a perpetual problem for religion. Many of the truths of religion deal with what we *ought* to do, the way we *ought* to be, and the kind of answers we *ought* to give to life's big questions. But the oughts cannot be understood until there has been some serious reflection on experience. A friend and I once came upon a huge arrangement of rocks alongside a hill, visible for miles, thousands of stones on the ground spelled out to read "Christ is the answer!" My companion, who was not a lover of slogans, could only remark, "But what was the question?"

None of the resurrection stories in the gospels begin with answers. They all begin with the women's wonder and fear, the disciples' confusion and doubt—qualities which the Baltimore Catechism hardly considered virtues. And yet, in the New Testament, these are the raw experiences out of which the disciples' lived experience of the risen Lord began to take shape.

This suggests that there is something very normal and indeed orthodox about the experience of confusion and doubt. It is hard to think of any profoundly lived experience—whether of pain and sorrow, or of joy and love—which does not begin with perplexity. There is a lesson here for all preachers and religion teachers who are tempted to come forward with answers before the raw experience of perplexity has been sufficiently savored and owned.

Story, the second element in the cycle, comes into play as raw experience becomes lived experience.

If you and I are friends who sit down to chat, and if we get talking about important things that have happened to each of us lately, invariably we will tell stories. But suppose you tell me about a friend who did something significant and loving for you, and I start philosophizing about the nature of friendship, with no touch of my own story in it. You will hardly resist looking at your watch and getting away as quickly as possible. Or if I share with you an experience of suffering that I am trying to own, and you answer with an analysis of the meaning of suffering, with little of yourself in it, I would barely resist telling you to go find a pulpit somewhere (which is not a happy comment on what goes on in pulpits). Not that there is anything wrong with philosophical discourse. It just belongs to another context.

Such examples indicate that we do not at first formulate our lived experiences into abstractions which provide firm answers. When an experience comes to have significance related to our lives, we put it into story form. Storytelling is our most spontaneous and basic way of *naming* an experience.

But we do not create our personal stories out of whole cloth, as though we name our experience in isolation from what goes on around us. We live in the midst of larger stories than our own personal story. We grow up with the larger stories of our family, the communities that surround us, the town and time in which we were born, our religious tradition, our nation, our western culture. Each of these groups provides us with its "myth," which is simply a name for each of the larger stories that surround and affect us. Each of these groups communicates its values to us, long before we even know how to reflect on the values communicated. Myths impinge upon us and frame our experience right from birth, shaping our attitudes long before we know what an attitude is. And the many myths surrounding us are often in competition.

We wear our myths like a suit of unmatched clothing. The task of life is to bring harmony into all this attire.

The process of owning our raw experience involves making choices, consciously and often only half-consciously, about what makes for meaning in our lives. In doing this, we tap into the larger stories that surround us. In one dimension of my life, I find myself drawn into the cultural myth of rugged individualism which encourages me to climb the ladder of worldly success. In another dimension, and at the other end of the spectrum, the story of Jesus shapes my meaning. In between, there are all the traditions of my communities and family: my Catholic religion, my Polish and German roots, my midwestern urban Americanism, and the values and priorities which I have inherited from my immediate family. Among all of these larger stories I pick and choose, with greater or lesser awareness, what makes for meaning. And so my suit of clothing is selected: my own story takes shape.

Scholars who talk about the principles of moral education do not take sufficient account of this dynamic. According to the norms of moral philosophy, decision-making must be rational. One must stick to logic and weigh all the facts. One must be autonomous, acting freely and not under compulsion. One must act according to moral principles which are universal; only the particular application changes. And so on. The elements that enter into a moral choice are variously described by different authors, but always one finds an emphasis on logic, rational abstraction, generality, and impersonal principles.[3]

Most people most of the time do not make choices, even the noblest and best of choices, on such impersonal grounds. True, one can always go back to look at a process of decision-making, and abstract the logical and generalized elements that figured into the process. But this analysis comes after the fact. The real world in which we make our choices includes imagination, creativity, old family programming, and countless non-rational factors that logical generalization can never account for. The vast majority of people make choices more out of the myths they live than out of the abstract principles they have learned. That is why it is so essential to become aware of the stories we live, the larger stories which we daily tap into and which give us the real backdrop for our most personal choices, good or bad.

There is a sad corollary to all of this. We are reminded today on all sides that many of us have no roots. We have become isolated from a whole variety of stories—familial, ethnic, religious, cultural. We are then left with the myth of TV sitcoms, we are seduced by the quality of life promoted by advertising, and we are paralyzed by the sensational pessimism of the daily news.

Roots are a patchwork of many myths. To have roots is to be wrapped in a cloak of many colors. But today, TV and the news and even the best of self-help books so overwhelm us with bits and pieces of competing myths that it is hard for any of us to put a unified shape on our raw experience. Minute scraps of cloth scattered around the house, the unfinished beginnings or the unresolved ends of human experiences, do not make a patchwork cloak. Only the pieces that are more whole, the larger stories, the myths provided by family and tradition and community shared, are big enough to be sewn into such a cloak, and to give worthwhile meaning to the raw experience of getting up in the morning and living through the day.

Lived experience and story are so closely linked that they finally become hard to distinguish. In the same way *story and festivity* go hand in hand, and it is difficult to separate them.

We need a context for storytelling, and festivity provides a pre-eminent one. Telling stories is an integral part of the festivity at a reunion or any other family celebration. Stories about Jesus were told and retold when the first Christians gathered for their celebrations—and there were many versions right from the beginning. It seems that a great many of the stories found in both the Old and New Testaments took shape in the context of worship. Were it not for religious festivity, many stories would not have been remembered and eventually written down. In our own families, few stories would be remembered if it were not for times of festivity.

The liturgy of the Word is a natural part of any religious celebration, because festivity calls for storytelling. The liturgy of the Word is the time when we tell our larger story in the hope of entering into it more fully in our own personal histories. (How often we treat this moment of liturgy as a time of instruction rather than a time of proclaiming and celebrating our story. That is why it is at times so boring and annoying.)

Even within the sacramental moments we turn to stories. At the heart of the eucharistic prayer is a story which tells why we are giving thanks and breaking bread in this way now. The blessing of water at baptism is also a story, telling of the waters of creation, the great flood, the Red Sea, the Jordan, the pierced side of Christ.

A ritual loses its moorings when it loses its story. An old man once told psychologist Carl Jung about one of the rituals of his African tribe. "In the morning, when the sun comes, we go out of the huts, spit into our hands, and hold them up to the sun." Jung asked the old man to describe the ceremony exactly. They held their hands in front of their mouths, spat or blew vigorously, then turned their palms upward toward the sun.

Jung asked what this meant, why they blew or spat into their hands, but he could not get an answer. "We've always done it," they said. Jung writes that "it was impossible to obtain any explanation, and I realized that they actually knew only *that* they did it, not *what* they were doing. They themselves saw no meaning in this action."4

I recently heard a story about a woman who, when she was preparing baked ham for dinner, always cut off the end of the ham before she put it into the oven. A friend of hers observed this one day and asked what it did for the flavor of the ham. "I'm not really sure," she answered. "My mother always did it." She later phoned her mother and asked her why she cut off the end of the ham, and her mother explained that Grandma always did it. Now really curious, the young woman phoned her grandmother and asked her what this did for the flavor of the ham. "Nothing that I know of," answered the grandmother. "The ham was usually too big for my roasting pan, so I cut off the end."

We all perform rituals without knowing why we do them. Why do we hide eggs on Easter? What do bunnies have to do with Easter? Why do we cut down trees and put them in our homes to dry out at Christmas time? Why do we hang stockings at Christmas? Why do we put candles on cakes? As in the case of the ham, we do not know where some of our ritual practices come from because we have lost the *story* that explains the ritual.

This is the problem that Paul was faced with, even during the earliest decades of the Christian experience. They were not perfect, those first followers of Jesus. Paul's letters remind us that an ideal church (thank God) has never existed. The community at Corinth, for example, was doing some singularly unchristian things when they met for the Lord's Supper. Some got drunk, and the more affluent were not sharing their food with the poor. And like some of those painful family gatherings we all know, where one person is in need and another talks only of how much he has made on the stock market, the Corinthians were split up into factions. Paul had to remind them that they were all together the Lord's own body. They should remember who they were as church, and recollect *why* they came together to break bread and share the cup (1 Cor 11).

Festivity had lost its moorings: the ritual had lost its story. So Paul had to remind the Corinthians of the story they had forgotten, "how on the same night that he was betrayed, the Lord Jesus took some bread, and thanked God for it and broke it, and said: This is my body which is for you." (We are so used to thinking of these words as "words of consecration" that it is hard to hear them as no more and no less than a *story*. It was centuries before anyone thought or spoke in terms of "words of consecration." Initially the whole thing is much simpler: The words of institution, like any story, *name* the action and proclaim why we are doing this now. More about this in the next chapter.)

The community at Corinth had similar troubles with baptism. It seems that people were forming cliques around the preachers who had baptized them, and they were narrowly identifying their faith with the particular message preached by the baptizing minister. Paul wrote at length about his understanding of the message, which he felt was being distorted. But at the heart of the matter lay the essential part of the story that gives the ritual of baptism its Christian meaning: You are baptized in the name of Jesus, not in the name of any church minister (1 Cor 1).

In his letter to Corinth, Paul is calling for a process of reflection which every age after him will have to carry on. Rituals like going into water or eating and drinking together are "plastic": they can take on any number of meanings. Paul's concern was that the community recognize the distinctive *Christian* meaning of their rituals.

"Remember your story, and so make sense of your rituals. Your festivity will then lead you further into the Christian experience." This is one way of summing up Paul's sacramental message to the Corinthians, and each age has to deal in its own way with the same admonition.

The situations that Paul was coping with have their parallels in everyday life. Festivity is one moment in a cycle, and unless the other elements of the cycle are at work, festivity is bound to lose its footing and its meaning. Everyone has had the experience of going to a gathering where there are all the externals of a celebration—people, food, drink, candles and cakes—and yet the feast is a flop.

Often this is because there is really nothing to celebrate. One need only think of the emptiness of many a New Year's Eve party. Particularly if Christmas has been well celebrated, New Year's Eve is more often an excuse for festivity than a natural opportunity within the flow of the cycle we have been looking at. Office parties can be similarly devastating, especially for the spouses of the employees. If there is no real story to share, or if no common lived experience lies behind the festivity, one is left with nothing but the trappings of festivity (and perhaps some desperate games).

Festivity is therefore never an end in itself. Festivity flows out of life and back into life. We always celebrate *something,* and that something is rooted in the first two elements of the cycle.

Another example of festivity detached from its natural cycle is a celebration which tries to substitute for a lived process. Families attempt this kind of thing when they use a celebration to cover over unhealed ruptures among members of the family. Again there are the external trappings of festivity: people and wine and a well-laid table. But if recognition of a rupture, then healing and reconciliation are needed among those who sit around the table, the feast can only be painful. Festivity in itself does not heal. It can and should celebrate a healing process which ought to have begun elsewhere.

For any church like the Catholic church whose tradition is so rich in ritual, there will always be the temptation of ritualizing without sufficient preparation. Theologians speak of the danger of "sacramentalizing without enough evangelizing." The problem here is nothing other than festivity detached from its natural human cycle.

The practice of sacramental confession is a good example. Confession has been plagued throughout its history with a narrow legalism that turns the celebration of God's mercy into a kind of coldly clinical legal pardon for unobeyed prescriptions. The decline of this sacrament—which few people associate with festivity!—owes much to our having recourse to it *before* some degree of reconciliation or healing has taken place, and before the mercy of God has been savored and experienced. The new *Rite of Penance* tries to put the sacramental moment back into its correct context: "Faithful Christians, *as they experience and proclaim the mercy of God in their lives,* celebrate with the priest the liturgy by which the church continually renews itself" (#11).

Can Catholic people and their pastors reverse the trend of centuries, and come to see the sacrament of penance in this marvelously festive way? I would urge that it cannot be done unless the people and their confessors are firmly in touch with their own experience and stories. If I may paraphrase a saying of G. K. Chesterton, the sacrament of penance hasn't failed; it mostly hasn't been tried.

If legalism is one fruit of a sacrament's becoming detached from its natural cycle, the magical attitude toward sacraments is another. It is well known that many Christians expect the sacraments to "do" something automatically for them, with only a minimal receptivity on their own part. More will be said about magic later, but it is easy enough to see how this attitude can be generated. Festivity always celebrates *something,* and that something is rooted in the first two elements of the cycle. Sacraments celebrate something, and that something has to do with the love of God, *experienced and related to one's own story.* If this element is absent, only magic is left. It is the same magic that some expect from a party where there is nothing to celebrate, or from a family feast that tries to substitute for a larger healing process.

When all three elements of the cycle are working in harmony, festivity has a precious role to play. Indeed, as I have been trying to suggest throughout this chapter, the rhythm of human life is simply incomplete without it. There are few experiences more depressing than being with people who never celebrate, either because they are "too busy" to make time for it, or (more depressing still) because they find nothing in their lives to celebrate.

If story *names* our lived experience, festivity *frames* it. We need to step back from the stories we are living, the history we are making, in order to see it all in a setting that makes it visible. Our lived experience and stories go on from day to day, like a flowing landscape with both bright and blighted spots. But we often miss the most striking points of the landscape, bright or blight, until we see it *framed* in a good photograph or painting. In the festive moment, we take a recess from the demands of story-making but without running from the story. In the sacramental moment, we take a breather from our story-making in order to frame and see better the stories we are living.

Festivity should not be understood only as a time of joy and laughter. Death needs to be celebrated, and that is why there are funeral rites. Mourning is a form of festivity which enables us to absorb the experience of death so that we can go on with life. Sickness is a profound experience that needs to be owned, and that is why there is a sacrament of the sick. Reconciliation after a rupture is often a long and painful process, but like sickness it is an experience that calls for a festive act. Celebration includes tears as well as laughter. Sometimes a good cry that wells from the heart is just the festive act that is needed to bring to term a portion of one's story, so that life can go on.

"Celebration," writes Harvey Cox, "reminds us that there is a side of our existence that is not absorbed in history-making, and therefore that history [including one's personal story] is not the exclusive or final horizon of life. As both an affirmation of history-making and a temporary respite from it, festivity reminds us of the link between two levels of our being—the instrumental, calculating side, and the expressive, playful side. Festivity periodically restores us to our proper relationship to history and history-making. It reminds us that we are fully within history but that history also is within something else."[5]

The "something else" within which our own histories lie is what the Christian sacraments want to hold open to our vision. This has to do with the "grace" of the sacrament, about which more will be said. But at this point we can say that a sacrament, like any festivity, wants to return us to everyday experience with a refreshed sense of the significance of one's own life. Is that not a profound "grace"?

Much more needs to be said about festivity, especially the

particular form of it which we call "sacrament." For the purposes of this chapter, I have been using words like *festivity, ritual,
celebration,* and *sacrament* quite interchangeably. Up to this point
I have simply wanted to propose a model and stimulate reflection on the different elements in the model.

The model is more than a model for sacramental theology.
The cycle we have been looking at also describes the *basics of religious education* at any stage. Religious education tries, through a
process of reflection, to raise people's raw experience to the level of lived experience. It tries to impart the story of the Christian
tradition and thus to give people a larger story, a cloak of many
colors, which can give meaning and shape to their own histories.
Finally—and this is a much neglected element in programs
which center too heavily on religious "instruction"—a good
program of religious education will teach people how to be festive. I would even urge that this is the end result of religious
education: people who know how to celebrate their love for one
another, and the mystery of God's love, at each stage of their experience. What subject in our school systems other than religious education can strive for this goal?

The model is also more than a religious model. The cycle
we have been studying is one way of describing the rhythm of
human life, or the rhythm that makes life human. If this cycle is
not actively at work in our normal lives, then we have lost or giv-
en up something of what makes life bearable. If this cycle is not
working, one has lost a firm touch with human *significance,* the
significance of being in this world and becoming human in it.

The story of the disciples on the road to Emmaus pulls together just about everything this chapter has talked about. As
Luke tells the story (Lk 24), these two men, along with so many
others, had recognized Jesus as a great prophet because of all
that he said and did in the sight of God and of the whole people.
It had been their hope that this man would be the one to set Is-

rael free. But it was their own priests and leaders who handed Jesus over to be sentenced to death.

The two disciples were stunned by the crucifixion, confused and hurt by the events of the preceding days. This was the raw experience. They talked about the raw experience until, with the Lord's help, they were drawn into reflection on how these events related to their own story. Then it became a *lived* experience. The Lord who walked with them took the *story* of the scriptures and explained to them how it was ordained that the Christ should suffer and so enter into his glory. The larger story made sense of their own immediate experience, and their hearts burned within them.

The end of the day brought sharing and a moment of celebration. The Lord sat with them at table, took bread and said the blessing, broke it and shared it with them. Their eyes were opened, and they recognized him. And this was *festivity.*

I have not tortured Luke's story or even rearranged it to make my point. The Emmaus incident simply brings into sharp focus the process by which we live, name, and frame our experience—the rhythm that makes life human.

asking the right question
chapter two

*T*he Roman church, along with other Christian churches, has a new set of sacramental rites. The commissions that worked on the new rites knew the basic questions to ask: What is the Easter experience that we are celebrating? How does each sacrament celebrate that experience? Where did the old rites miss the mark? Are there parts of the story we have been overlooking?

But revising books is easier than revising people. We have now become aware of the substantial changes in thinking and attitude that need to go along with the new books. Turning altars around, talking English, having laypeople read at Mass and distribute communion, hearing confessions in a pleasant room instead of a dark box—only a few years ago such things looked like radical reform. Indeed they were at the time, but it is now evident to a vast number of Catholics that all of this has only been a scratch on the surface.

Attitudes are not reformed merely by external changes, or by changes in the elements of festivity. We have to develop new attitudes toward the whole cycle of experience and story as well.

The fact is that for centuries we had been living on a tradition, a story, which was too narrow and not sufficiently "catholic," not expressive enough of our whole tradition. Especially where the sacraments are concerned, we had been living mostly on the ideas handed down to us from the middle ages. And the insights of the middle ages are not the whole story. In order to be truly catholic and universal, we have to take into account a whole two thousand years, not just a few centuries. The Second Vatican Council was in touch with much modern research which put us into fuller contact with our past and with older sources that had been overlooked or forgotten. This council's message to the church, especially in the area of liturgy and sacrament, was that it is time to pick up where the Council of Trent left off in the sixteenth century, at the end of the middle ages.

This is not a simple issue. A century ago Pope Leo XIII insisted that all theologizing must harmonize with the conclusions of Thomas Aquinas, a man of the thirteenth century. Until very recent decades, Catholic publishing reflected this enthronement of the middle ages. I remember a book entitled *The Thirteenth, the Greatest of Centuries.*

Today's Catholics who are over forty—laypeople who went to Catholic colleges, their pastors who studied in seminaries, and those less schooled who learned their Catholicism from pulpit and catechism—all were imbued with a view of history which saw the middle ages as the golden age of religious understanding. Scripture and the writings of the church fathers during the early centuries were considered vague, unsharpened, or insufficiently clarified until men like Aquinas came along. Since then, according to this view, there has been mostly decline, and the best theology is a repetition or rewording of medieval insights, filtered through the Council of Trent.

Many Catholics no longer accept the perspective that the insights of one era should be normative for all ages. Others are disturbed to see this perspective called into question, and some functionaries in the church are determined to keep it alive and healthy. But the fact remains that Vatican II officially opened the door onto a modern interpretation of history in which the past is not absolutized and each era is permitted its own insights.

Medieval theology had many limitations, because it worked against heavy odds. The four or five centuries which we call the Dark Ages (roughly 600–1000 A.D.) were a crude age, a time when sheer self-preservation was practically the only concern of people. Even monasteries were rough places; among the monks were warlords who had been sent to a monastery because they had gotten into trouble with the king or emperor. Such practices were not calculated to make the monastery a center of study and learning. When the great medieval universities began to develop in the twelfth century, the vast majority of people thought the world was flat, even though fifteen centuries earlier the Greeks knew it wasn't.

The Spirit was still at work in the church, preserving the faith of the church. There were still holy people during the Dark Ages. But there was little learning, and a great deal of information about the past and about our Christian origins was simply lost. The theologians of the thirteenth century did remarkable work in recovering and reformulating insights that had become obscure during the Dark Ages. But especially in the area of worship and the sacraments, they lacked basic historical information.

For example, medieval theologians did not know that Jesus created no new rituals. They did not know that a meal of bread and wine was already a religious practice before Jesus' time. They did not know that the practice of individual confession went back only to the sixth century, not anywhere near the time of Jesus. They did not know that confirmation was separated from baptism more by accident than by design. In the middle ages, the anointing of the sick had become last rites for those who were dying. There was "extreme unction," a sacrament for those departing from this life, but there was no sacrament of the *sick* and no real theology for it. As for holy orders, the scholastics were not agreed whether the episcopate was a sacrament or only an honor added to the priesthood. They did not know that it was several centuries before presbyters began taking over from bishops sacramental duties like presiding at the eucharist.

In short, much information which any well-informed Catholic today takes for granted was simply not available to the theologians of the middle ages. So it is not surprising that their sacramental theology does not reflect the whole of the Christian tradition. Key parts of the story were missing along with important dimensions of lived experience. This inevitably affected reflection on the meaning of the sacraments. Not that we now have to reject what the medievals did, but we do have to take account of what they overlooked or simply did not know about the tradition. It is a matter of broadening our understanding, seeing the larger or more universal story, and so becoming more authentically "catholic."

Today, when we talk about "celebrating baptism" or "celebrating the eucharist," we are using quite a different language from the one most of us learned as children. It is important to reflect on the language we use, because the way we talk usually mirrors the way we think about things. "Celebrating the eucharist" represents an attitude that is quite different from "saying and hearing Mass."

The new language is not arbitrary. It reflects important discoveries that we have made about our origins. When the early Christians came together for worship, they were very conscious of themselves as a community gathered in the name of their Lord Jesus. Different people performed different roles in their rituals. But the people were conscious that the whole celebration was *their* action, not just the action of the presiding ministers.

Suppose you were a Christian early in the second century.

What would you do on Sunday morning? Let's set the scene as though it were a North American city, where you live, say, on the near west side. Though this is Sunday, the Lord's day for Christians, it is an ordinary working day, not a day of rest. So the Christian community has to gather before the working day begins. You and your family get up around five in the morning. You set out through the quiet streets as the sun is rising. In your pocket or purse you carry a small bun which you will bring to the eucharistic table.

You pass by what is now Saint Augustine's and Central Presbyterian. They weren't churches then. At that time they were temples dedicated to Democracy and Free Enterprise (a good enough modern equivalent for Jupiter and Apollo). You walk through a neighborhood of large houses until you come to a house owned by a Christian family. You slip in the back door of the house, and a man looks you over as you come in. (You belong to an illegal organization, and you are risking a death sentence or at least life in a penal colony by coming to this assembly.) The man, who is one of the deacons of your church, recognizes you and greets you.

You walk into the large living room, which looks just as it does any other day. But now it is filling up with people; the church is assembling. It is a very mixed group socially, economically, racially; there are people from every part of town. You know most of them by name, but the ones you know best are people from your own neighborhood, because you meet with them in small groups during the week for prayer, or instruction, or reflection on the writings of the apostles. (You have never heard the term "New Testament." It would still be decades until that term was devised to cover the apostolic writings. You are probably familiar with most of Paul's letters, and perhaps a few of the gospels. Chances are that you don't know all four gospels; it would still be a while before all of these writings circulated in all of the communities.)

Everyone is standing around chatting. Someone comes over
to you and introduces a young couple, friends from another city.
They brought along with them a loaf from last Sunday's eucharist: the Christian community in their town asked them to bring
it as a sign of unity among the churches.

You are happy to see Ned O'Neil and John Kubicek shaking
hands and embracing. There are tears of happiness and relief in
Judy Kubicek's eyes. The two men had gotten into a severe argument not long ago, and both had been missing from the eucharistic assembly for several weeks. A saying of Jesus is coming
alive before your eyes: "If you bring your gift to the altar and
there recall that your brother has anything against you, leave
your gift at the altar, go first to be reconciled with your brother,
and then come and offer your gift" (Mt 5:23–24).

At the other end of the living room sits an older man. This
is the bishop of your city, the head pastor. He is dressed like any
of the other men in the room; no one wears any unusual clothing. At the moment he is talking to a few of the men who are
seated near him, in a semicircle facing down the room. These
are the "elders" or "presbyters" of your community, the men in
charge of the community's affairs, much like a parish council. (In
your community there might be some women among these presbyters. Documents from the second century indicate that women
were not universally excluded from this form of leadership until
later.)

The celebration is about to begin. The bishop stands and
greets the whole assembly, and all of you reply to his greeting.
Then you turn and embrace your neighbor warmly. Perhaps you
go over and give the kiss of peace to someone whom you haven't
seen for a while (there are no pews to get in your way). This is a
kiss, a real embrace. People who are risking a sentence of death
in order to come together tend to greet one another with something a bit warmer than a formal handshake.

In front of the bishop is a small table. Two deacons stand in

front of it (one might be a woman), one holding a silver plate
and the other a two-handled silver cup. You all file up and put
the bun you brought with you on the plate, and then you pour a
little wine into the cup. The plate and cup are placed on the table in front of the bishop, and some water is added to the cup.

Then the bishop and elders stand with their hands outstretched over the bread and cup. They do this in silence, letting
the gesture speak for itself. It is a gesture you recognize well,
this "laying on of hands." It occurs in nearly every ritual you
have ever experienced. When you were preparing to become a
Christian, your teacher laid hands on you at the end of every
session. This commonest of Christian gestures is now being
used to focus your attention on the bread and wine, which will
be broken and shared in order to "speak" who you all are as
church: the Lord's own body.

Then the bishop invites you to lift up your hearts, and to
give thanks to the Lord our God. You answer, sharing in the in-
troductory dialogue which is one of the oldest elements of the
Christian liturgy. His hands still outstretched over the bread and
cup, the bishop then chants a short prayer, giving thanks for creation, God's care for us, and our re-creation as a new people re-
deemed in Christ. It is a short prayer, very simple, much shorter
than our present eucharistic prayers.

After the prayer of thanksgiving the bishop breaks one of
the buns and eats a piece of the loaf. He then takes three sips
from the cup. Meanwhile the two deacons break the other
loaves. You watch this action in silence, aware that these pieces
of bread broken from single loaves speak of the unity of Christians in one body.

The bishop stands in front of the table with the plate of
broken bread. You go up to him and he says to you, "The bread
of heaven in Christ Jesus." You answer "Amen," taking a piece
of bread in your hands. You eat the bread, and then go over to
the deacon who offers you the silver cup. He says to you, "In

God the Father almighty." You answer "Amen" and take your
first sip from the cup. (This assembly takes its time with communion, because the action is the central thing.) You take your second and third sips after the deacon has said "In the Lord Jesus
Christ" and finally "In the Holy Spirit in the holy church."

You go back to your place, and there is a pause for prayer as
everyone finishes communicating. Many of you go up to the
bishop again with a little silver box. He puts some fragments of
the bread in the box, which you put into your pocket or purse.
This is for members of your family who could not come this
morning, perhaps because of illness. (This is the origin of reserving the eucharistic bread after the celebration. The practice
began not for purposes of adoration, but for the sake of the sick
or the absent.)

The bishop then dismisses the gathering, perhaps with a
short prayer or blessing. You return home, hoping you won't be
stopped by the police and caught with that little silver box on
you. You have your breakfast and then begin the working day.
That evening, or some other time during the week, you will
meet with one or another small group in your neighborhood,
for prayer and reflection.

That's what it would have been like. The whole thing was
very simple and brief, quite unimpressive to an outsider. I do
not want to romanticize the group of people assembled in that
living room. They were generally very dedicated, but they had
their conflicts and problems just as we have ours. Paul's letters
and other early documents are reminders that there were serious conflicts and doctrinal disagreements even in the earliest
communities.

But the experience of the eucharist was, for them, different
from what our modern experience has usually been. Their attitude toward the sacraments was the original Christian attitude,
which can be summed up this way: *The sacraments are actions, not
things.* They are actions which the assembly performs, not

"things" which we "receive." They are something *we do* rather than something that is done *to us.*

Unfortunately, this sense of being the Lord's own body and celebrating it receded as the centuries went by. This began happening in the fourth century, after Constantine, when Christianity was suddenly no longer an illegal organization but the emperor's own religion. Your social standing and even your success in the business world came to depend on your being a Christian. If you were one of the men assembled in that second-century living room, you could not be a soldier. Soldiers have to kill, and Christians were total pacifists. But a few centuries later you couldn't get anywhere in the military *unless* you were a Christian. In other words, membership in the church came to be one of the credit cards you had to carry if you were to be successful in the world.

The church was originally a *we,* a group of people with a strong common awareness of being one in Christ. Gradually the church became an *it,* an organization to belong to. Note how the understanding of church and of sacrament go hand in hand:

The sacraments are actions, not things.

The church is a we, not an it.

If someone in that living room had spoken to you of "ministry," you would not first have thought of the bishop or presbyters or deacons at the other end of the room. You would spontaneously have applied the word to yourself. Everyone had a ministry, because everyone had gifts from the Lord which were brought to the service of the community. But gradually the whole sense of a corporate venture, involving a variety of gifts all contributing to the upbuilding of the one body, was lost. The word "ministry" came to be restricted to people holding full-time positions of leadership in the community. If you were not one of those fulltimers, you came to think of the "church" more and more as something out there, something else, someone other than yourself.

This of course is where some Christians are today. The church is like a credit card. It is more an institution than an assembly of believers. It is more a thing than an activity, and the word "church" itself evokes a building rather than people. If, when you hear that word, the first thing that comes to mind is people rather than a building, it is only because you have given much time and effort to the work of overcoming old attitudes.

The loss of awareness of *being church* brought with it a decline in sacramental practice. Communion was no longer an essential part of the eucharistic action for most people, and the sacraments were no longer an action in which the whole assembly felt engaged. They came to be seen as the priest's action, something done *to us* rather than something *we do*.

The sacraments thus became "things" which you "went to church" (the building) to "receive," and a whole new way of talking about the sacraments developed. In the early church (the assembly, not the building), all of the faithful were "celebrators." That was the word used in various languages to describe Christians engaged in worship. But by the beginning of the middle ages, the faithful had become simply "recipients." The thing-mentality took over entirely, and it was summed up in the idea that the sacraments will "take effect" on you just so long as you don't "place an obstacle" in their way.

How the eucharist turned from an action into a thing is well illustrated by what happened to the words of institution. In the middle of the prayer of thanksgiving is a *story*, an account of the last supper. The story appears there because it tells why we are giving thanks in just this way with bread and wine. The story is addressed to people who are engaged in doing what Jesus said we should do. But as the people became "recipients" rather than "celebrators," the words came to be addressed, by the priest bent low over the bread and cup, to the objects to be received.

Most people, when they are asked what are the eucharistic symbols, will answer "Bread and wine." (What answer did *you* just give?) That is the answer that medieval theology gave. Bread and wine are the matter of the sacrament, the words of institution are the form. But the original eucharistic symbols are actions, not things. The original eucharistic symbols are *breaking the bread and sharing the cup.*

We are so affected by the thing-mentality that it is hard for us to hear the story of the last supper. "This is my body," said the Lord, and for centuries we have heard the word "this" as referring to the bread. Listen to the text again, with the attitude of sacrament as action rather than thing, and the story will have a different ring. Jesus took bread, *said a blessing, broke the bread and gave it* to his disciples, saying "This is my body which is *given for you.*"

The "body which is given for you" is symbolized in the whole action of blessing, breaking and sharing the bread. The word "this" refers to the *whole action,* not to the bread alone.

The New Testament gives different accounts of the last supper. Paul and Luke include the relational phrase for the bread; Matthew and Mark do not; all four give a relational phrase for the cup ("my blood which is poured out for you"). The old Roman Canon did not contain the phrase "given for you," and it did not figure into scholastic theology's concept of the essential form of the sacrament. It is for good reason that the new Roman rite has restored the phrase. Are not the *relational* words essential for naming the exact sense of what Jesus was doing?

Medieval stress on the things of the eucharist changed the focus of theology and catechetics. When we who are the inheritors of the object-mentality talk about the eucharist today, our first question tends to be "What happens to the bread and wine?" The answer is that it is changed, and we are taught that the medieval theory known as "transubstantiation" is the most fitting explanation of the change. A vast number of Catholics have become uncomfortable with this explanation because it has the ring of magic. Here I will only remark that the theory of transubstantiation is understandable in its historical context. It is a reasonable explanation in the terms of a philosophy of substance. The difficulty is that the theory is intrinsically tied to the object-mentality. As such, the theory of transubstantiation is a good answer to a bad question.[6]

The question that eventually generated the theory of transubstantiation—What happens to the bread and wine?—does not appear in theological writings until the ninth century. The earlier Christian tradition did not think of Christ's presence or of the eucharistic "change" in terms of the objects of bread and wine alone. For the church fathers, what is said about the objects has to be said also about the *people*. Their preoccupation can be put this way: "What happens to the people who celebrate with bread and wine?"

Their answer, as someone like Augustine put it, was that we must *be* what we have eaten. We already are the body of Christ, but we must *become* that body still more so. We have to be bread for others, just as Jesus is bread given for us. Christ is our passover, but the passover should also be happening *in us*. If our food and drink is the Lord himself, the important thing is that sharing this food makes us "pass over" into what we have eaten, so that "everywhere we carry him with whom we are dead, buried, and raised to life." Those are the words of Leo the Great. John Chrysostom is even more vivid. Through the food the Lord has given us, we become "members of his flesh and of his bones." We are "mixed into" that flesh, and he has "kneaded his body with ours."

Ideas like these, which fill the sermons and writings of the church fathers, express the earliest tradition of the church. What is said of the worshiping faithful goes hand in hand with what is said of the bread and wine: this body given *for you.* Someone once asked, in a course I was teaching on the eucharist, why I never referred to the "sacred" host and the "precious" blood. It occurred to me that when the church fathers use adjectives of this kind—and they do it often—in the same breath they invariably talk about the sacred and precious *people* who are celebrating the sacrament.

The loss of awareness of "being church" brought with it a loss of this sense of our own sacredness. Theology's shift of attention from people to things both reflected this loss and fostered it. What began in medieval theology became a hardened tradition in the centuries following the Council of Trent, when Catholic theology was preoccupied with defending its tradition against Protestant attacks on it. Little theological reflection was given to the church as the holy priesthood and consecrated people spoken of in scripture and so richly elaborated by the fathers. In the writings of those centuries the sacredness of the Christian people seemed to become almost totally projected onto the eucharistic objects of bread and wine.

There were profound pastoral consequences here. One need only think of many of our parents and grandparents who took communion very rarely, and who would spend weeks preparing for the event. Implicit here was the attitude that we are sinners who come to the sacraments in order to receive a holy thing. It is the sacrament that is sacred and holy; we are not.

The problem is not the holiness of the sacraments but rather our attitude toward ourselves. There are important insights in the medieval tradition which we can profit from, and which will be mentioned in due course. There were also moments of liturgical renewal during the centuries we have been surveying. At the moment I am stressing the negative fruits of this tradition in order to emphasize the unhappy attitudes that can be generated when theology asks the wrong questions. It should be clear at this point that for many centuries the sacramental question has been put the wrong way around. The "things" of the sacraments can make sense only if our reflection begins not with the things, but with the people and their action.

from
symbol
to   *chapter three*
sacrament

handwritten margin note: "sacrament" / mystery

Doctrine takes time to develop. We first tell our lived experiences in story and celebrate them in festivity. Logical analysis and systematic concepts come much later, after much further reflection.

Recall for a moment the scene described in the last chapter: a group of people assembled for the eucharist in someone's living room, sometime during the second century. If you were to ask any of those people about their "sacraments," they would not have known what you meant. They could talk to you about the meaning of baptism or the breaking of the bread, and of course they had names for each of their rituals. But it took centuries before a *generalized* concept like "sacrament" was developed to cover all such rituals.

The process here is normal enough. We do things long before we generalize about the nature of what we are doing. Scientists in their laboratories observe a phenomenon and spend days or even years isolating it before they can generalize and give it a name. In the sacramental realm, Christians lived their symbols long before they began exploring *how* and *why* outward symbols signify inward things. It is not surprising that the earliest generalized definition of a sacrament, which comes to us from Augustine (+430), does little more than state the connection between symbol and the reality signified. A sacrament, he says, is a "visible form of invisible grace."

430 AD

The early Christians knew very well, if they ever wanted to put it into words, that their outward rituals signified something spiritual. Augustine's generalization would not have surprised them. Augustine himself did not dream that he was uttering the elements of a definition which was destined to become famous. He was simply explaining in one of his letters how the fruit of a Christian ritual does not depend on the moral character of the minister. The minister, he wrote, deals only with the "visible form" of the sacrament; God alone is responsible for the "invisible grace." Augustine was not engaging in a methodical reflection on the meaning of sacrament. He was simply answering a pastoral question.[7]

But Augustine's writings were an important resource for subsequent centuries, even his correspondence with its comments on occasional questions. In any dispute Augustine came to be considered a weighty authority. As time passed and new questions came up, theologians kept repeating Augustine's "definition" of sacrament, elaborating on it and working it in with their own theological perspectives. We inherit the definition, filtered through the middle ages, the Council of Trent and post-Tridentine scholastic theology, in the form that is well known to any Catholic: Sacraments are "outward signs instituted by Christ to give grace."

The definition as we have inherited it is much more restrictive than Augustine's formula. In his own list of sacraments, Augustine included many actions and things which he considered "visible forms of invisible grace": the kiss of peace, the font of baptism, the blessed salt, the creed, the Lord's Prayer, the ashes of penance. Augustine's formula defines a *symbol,* not just the particular symbolic actions that we call by the name of sacraments. I will come back to this point later. For the moment all we need to note is this first stage of generalization associated with the word "sacrament."

As time passed there was more and more concern with naming those rituals which are at the center of the church's life. There are many signs of holy things, many visible forms of invisible grace, but which things and rituals are "efficacious"? That is, which rituals carry with them the guarantee of God's grace?

This was the question that preoccupied the medieval schoolmen. Along with the refining of a generalized definition of sacrament came an enumeration of those particular rites that could be fittingly included in the list. The number seven was not reached all at once. Hugh of St.Victor, who died in 1141, discussed Augustine's definition and put many nuances on it, but he still included a good many "visible forms of invisible grace" in his list of sacraments: holy water, liturgical vessels and vestments, the dedication of churches, and (significantly for Vatican II and the theology of our own time) the incarnation of Jesus and the church itself as the body of Christ.

Peter Abelard, a contemporary of Hugh, enumerated six sacraments, omitting holy orders. (We shall see later how orders and matrimony are sacraments in a different sense from the other five.) By the time of Peter Lombard, who died just twenty years after Hugh and Abelard (1161), theologians seemed to be agreeing on the list of seven. This agreement was reflected in the canons of local church councils in the late 1100's and early 1200's.

How was this agreement on the number seven reached? A number of factors seemed to be pulling together at once. Under the influence of the new blossoming of dialectics and philosophy after the dark ages, theologians became more and more concerned with accurate generalization and definition of familiar realities. They were reflecting, with new tools for reflection, on the lived experience of their time. With the new or rediscovered tools of logic and philosophy, they were trying to understand the pastoral life of the church in a coherent way.

A distinction between "sacraments" and "sacramentals" did not exist before the twelfth century, but it was inevitable that it should be created. It was clear, then as now, that some visible forms of invisible grace are more important than others. The seven rituals which the schoolmen agreed on as "sacraments" were in fact rituals that were common to all of the churches and transcended local differences. Even the eastern churches could and did accept this enumeration. Finally, as the scholastics liked to point out, it was "fitting" that there should be seven sacraments, because seven is a number which symbolizes wholeness.

The New Testament and the practice of the *early* church had little to do with the numbering of the seven. Baptism and the eucharist are of course amply discussed in the New Testament. But the medievals also tried to find in the pages of the gospels the precise moments when Christ "instituted" each of the other sacraments. The sacrament of Christian marriage, it was argued, was instituted at the wedding feast of Cana (Jn 2). Holy orders and the sacrament of penance were instituted when, on Easter eve, Jesus appeared to the disciples, breathed on them (therefore "ordained" them), and sent them forth with the commission to forgive sins (Jn 20).

Modern scholarship does not accept this kind of proof-texting because it is now evident that the New Testament writers were addressing different questions from those which the medieval schoolmen were trying to answer. In fact, the early church's commentaries on such biblical texts are in accord with the conclusions of modern biblical scholarship. The story of the marriage at Cana has to do with the banquet of the messianic kingdom and with Christ's bringing the new messianic wine— not with the Christian institution of marriage. The appearance to the disciples on Easter eve has to do with the whole mission of the church and its proclamation of God's love and forgiveness—not simply with the rituals of holy orders or penance as we know them. It is also clear to us now, as it was not clear to the schoolmen of the middle ages, that the ritual practices of the early church were understood and organized in a different way from those of the medieval church.

Scholastic theologians themselves detected problems here, both during and after the middle ages, because they discussed distinctions between "direct" and "indirect" institution of the sacraments by Christ. In any case, the numbering of the seven sacraments did not come out of reflection on biblical data or the life of the early church. It came from the actual liturgical practice of the medieval church and observation of what was universal in practice, with some influence from the fitting symbolism of the number seven.

On the eve of the Reformation, two main points of doctrine or generalization about the sacraments had evolved. First, there was agreement that certain rituals must be considered "efficacious" forms of grace. Even if the minister is sinful, certain rituals are guaranteed in a special way by God. They "effect the grace which they signify," and it is the Lord, not ourselves, who causes this grace. Second, there was agreement that seven rituals belonged to this category: baptism, confirmation (now, but not originally, a separate rite from baptism), the eucharist, penance (now exclusively, but not originally, individual confession), extreme unction (now a sacrament of the dying, not a sacrament for the sick), matrimony and holy orders (now seen more as rites than as ministries or ways of living).

Other things and rites which an earlier tradition considered as sacraments in accord with Augustine's definition (the kiss of peace, the baptismal font, holy water, vestments, etc.) remained visible forms of invisible grace. But such "sacramentals" (a new term) could not be said to carry the guarantee of grace: they do not ineluctably effect what they signify.

Although the language surrounding the sacraments had now become physicalist to an extreme, not all theologians failed to nuance their way of expressing how the sacraments cause grace. Aquinas, for example, abandoned the phrase *ex opere operato* in his last writings (the phrase is a piece of technical Latin jargon which implies that the sacraments take effect "automatically," and indeed it is hard to translate the phrase in any other way). Behind the physicalist language that gave power to the "things" of the sacraments, there still lay the point which the better theologians of that age were most interested in getting across. The point can be expressed easily enough in less magical, more biblical language: Certain rites of the church should be seen as privileged expressions of the covenant between the Lord and his church.

The Reformation did not call this principle into question. In the sixteenth century it was the number of sacraments, not the sacramental principle itself, that became the problem. In an age when sacramental practices had become tied up with abuses like indulgences and superstitious guarantees of salvation, the reformers wanted to get back to biblical simplicity and to the norms of the early church. The medievals had used biblical texts to support their numbering of seven sacraments. The new textual criticism of the Renaissance called many of these arguments into question, and the Bible could no longer be used to validate all of the sacramental practices of the day. What should be done?

In general, the Protestant reformers agreed that the term "sacrament" should be restricted to those rituals which Christ commanded to be observed, and to which he gave a promise of grace. All agreed that baptism and the eucharist fulfilled this criterion. As to the other five sacraments, opinions differed. Calvin and Zwingli rejected them out of hand as spurious ceremonies. Luther and Melancthon on the other hand were sympathetic toward penance, which they saw related to baptism. Luther also saw spiritual and pastoral value in the rites of confirmation and extreme unction. Though these rites were not commanded by Christ and cannot be called "sacraments" in the strict sense, they remain useful and even very healing "ceremonies."

The Reformation opened a new phase in the process of doctrinal development concerning the sacraments. Primacy had always been given to baptism and the eucharist, and the schoolmen made distinctions among those sacraments that were "necessary for salvation" and those that were not. Several medieval theologians had subordinated holy orders and marriage to the other sacraments because, unlike the other five, these two are not for all the faithful. When the reformers insisted on distinguishing between the two biblical sacraments (baptism and eucharist) and other rituals which are not endowed with a specific command of Christ, they exposed questions which theology had not dealt with in any depth. How are the sacraments related to one another? Above all, how is each of the traditional seven related to the life of the *church*?

Unfortunately, the sixteenth century did not manage to formulate these questions thoroughly and accurately, much less explore them. As the Reformation evolved, most Protestant churches lost touch with the lived experience of many sacraments. They increasingly abandoned all rites which Jesus had not explicitly commanded in the gospels. Even the eucharist was less and less frequently celebrated, as reaction to medieval abuses and emphasis on faith and hearing the Word led to a rabid anti-sacramentalism in most Protestant communities.

Catholicism responded to all of this at the Council of Trent by reaffirming the authority and traditions of the church. This council had to deal with a morass of needed reforms, and it is not surprising that the quality of its work was uneven. Trent's decree on grace and justification is a remarkably balanced piece of theology. On the other hand the decrees on the sacraments, issued in different sessions of the council over a spread of fifteen years (1547–1563), dealt more with practical abuses than with the articulation of a cohesive theology.

On theological grounds, Trent did little more than reaffirm the sacramental principle and re-enumerate the sacraments. There are seven efficacious sacraments, said the council, no more and no less. An explicit command of Christ is not required for authenticity; one must not reject a tradition on scriptural grounds alone. Trent reasserted the *fact* of the sacraments without exploring the interrelationship or subordination among them, or the relationship of all the sacraments to the life of the church.

It was left for the twentieth century to pick up this phase of doctrinal evolution. A very critical development took place in our century as theologians turned to reflection on the nature of the church. As we saw earlier, a reflective sense of being church existed in the early Christian centuries; and it was in this context that rituals and sacraments were understood, namely as expressions of the church and its life in Christ. But this sense of being church waned, and by the middle ages the church had come to be defined in legalistic and institutional terms. Thus, by the time a formal theology of the *sacraments* was elaborated, there was no longer a well-articulated theology of the *church* to underpin it.

In the sixteenth century neither Catholics nor Protestants possessed the theology that is so familiar to us now, namely that the *church itself* is the core sacrament, as Christ is himself the sacrament of God. Prior to any other enumeration of the sacraments, Christ and his people are the first "visible form of invisible grace." Today the idea of being church has become the starting point for all sound sacramental theology. In this perspective, our rituals are sacramental because we the church, with Christ, are the core sacrament, celebrating in many ritual forms the grace and love of God.

Our age has picked up still another question which the past had left unexplored. Theology faithfully maintained that the sacraments are "outward signs," but it never developed a thorough explanation of the exact meaning of sign or symbolic reality. In fact, a good many Catholic catechisms virtually denied the traditional definition which they asserted. Having stated that the sacraments are outward signs, they went on to explain that the eucharist is not *just* a sign but *really* the body and blood of Christ.

What are symbols for? How are they related to reality? What do symbols mean, and what do they do? For the past thousand years Christian theology answered such questions only in terms of the seven sacraments. In our time, scholars have looked into the larger question of what *any good symbol* means and what it does. The early Christians celebrated going into the water, breaking the bread, anointing with oil, laying on hands; they savored the blessed salt, they exchanged the kiss of peace, they treasured the font of baptism. All of these actions and things were "visible forms of invisible grace," and when Augustine named them as such, he was doing no more and no less than defining a good *symbol*. Later ages would work other definitions out of Augustine's formula. But the fact is that the sacraments *are* symbols: this is where the theology of the sacraments began, and it is where our own age has had to return.

The problem for us is that the sacraments have become so "churchy," so separated from the lives we live at home and at work and at play, that we no longer spontaneously relate them to the other symbols that surround and affect us. The middle ages asked: What do sacraments do, and how are they efficacious? We now have to ask a larger question: What do *symbols* do, and how are they efficacious?

Symbols do what abstract thought cannot do. Symbols bring us into touch with realities which are at once familiar and mysterious. We use symbols to bring into our heads and hearts realities which are intimate to us, but which always lie beyond the power of our heads to pigeon-hole and absorb into abstract ideas. Augustine spoke of visible forms of invisible grace. The same idea can be put in a more contemporary way: Symbols are tangible, and when we touch them we touch a mystery that is at once familiar and elusive.

The love between a man and his wife is familiar; it is present to them day in and day out. Yet it remains a mystery, because any love defies rational analysis. For some couples wedding rings might be a reminder of an ideal love, a love that never came to be, or a romantic love that has faded. For a couple who possess their present love, the rings are a carrier of something real and present. Worn and felt and noticed at various moments of the day, the rings are symbols of the familiar mystery which the wife and husband are living. Don't such things as rings touch into a familiar mystery?

The covenant between Yahweh and his people was a familiar reality for the Israelites, but like any love it exceeded the mind's ability to abstract and rationalize. On one solemn occasion when the tribes of Israel were called together to renew their commitment to their Lord, Joshua took a great stone and set it up under the oak tree in the sanctuary of the Lord (Josh 24:27). He named that stone as a symbol of the covenant the people had renewed, the familiar mystery they had chosen to live. Afterward, could anyone see or touch that stone without being touched?

Life and fertility, strength and courage, wisdom and gentleness are abstract words for other familiar mysteries. The Indian tribes of North America used animals and birds and fish to symbolize the energies and values that were most central to their existence, their struggles and happiness and hopes. Composed into a totem pole, these different figures are a powerful expression of the identity of an Indian nation, of the familiar mystery that the nation experiences and lives. Why are we touched, quite irrationally, when we see a totem?

Flags and emblems serve the same purpose for modern folk. Our nation's flag symbolizes a reality that is no less familiar and no less mysterious than the forces of nature: people working together to form a society, *e pluribus unum*, with the goal of freedom and justice for all. Why are we moved, again quite irrationally, when our nation's flag is carried in parade?

We use symbols like stones and wedding rings, totems and flags and emblems, precisely because they *work* where logic or a sermon does not. Symbols, not discourses or discussions, do the most effective job of bringing into our awareness the realities of loving and being alive, living and struggling and dying together. The best discussions we have are invariably the ones that bring us closer into touch with these familiar mysteries, the mysteries that are exposed to us by all the symbols of living and struggling and dying that surround us. Any of these familiar mysteries are "invisible graces" which we spontaneously express to ourselves in visible forms, whether it be rings or stones or flags or the breaking of bread.

Augustine's classic definition of a sacrament thus applies no less to a wedding ring than it does to the water of baptism. This was no problem for Augustine or for any of the early fathers, but it became a problem as later theologians sought more precision about the meaning of the Christian sacraments. As sacramental theory evolved, the sacraments became so thoroughly distinguished *from* other symbols that the very notion of *symbol* no longer did the job of describing what the sacraments were about.

The best illustration of this is the dispute that took place over the eucharist in the eleventh century, which I alluded to earlier and which has reverberated into the catechisms of our own day. The two sides argued whether the eucharistic elements were "only a symbol" or whether they were "really" the body and blood of Christ. Symbol and reality, symbol and the familiar mystery, were no longer in the kind of harmony I described above. Symbol had come to mean something *other than* the reality which it signified, something vague.

Orthodoxy was forced to insist on the reality of Christ's presence in the eucharist, but it was crippled in two ways. First, as we saw earlier, the whole question was now put in terms of the elements of the eucharist, the things of the sacrament rather than the action, the bread and wine rather than the breaking of the bread and the sharing of the cup. Second, in a climate where the idea of symbol had come to mean a mere reminder of reality, not a "realizer" of reality, no one investigated the meaning of what a symbol does. In the absence of a philosophy of symbol, the medieval schoolmen turned to the Greek philosophy of substance to affirm the reality of Christ's presence in the eucharistic elements; the reality was affirmed by maintaining that the substance of the bread and wine is changed. It did not occur to anyone to ask whether "substance" is in fact the most helpful category for understanding symbolic realities like the sacraments.

Any symbol can degenerate into a mere reminder. A flag can become a nostalgic reminder of a glorious past, and wedding rings can become reminders of a sweeter and more romantic love that existed on the day of the wedding. Perhaps some people coming to Shechem a generation after Joshua saw the stone he placed under the oak tree as a mere reminder of a more fervent moment in their history. But when symbols are only reminders, *they are no longer symbols.* A real symbol always brings us into touch not just with a memory but with a living present, and indeed a present which contains a hope for the future and which helps to carry us into the future.

Traditional theology worried that the sacraments, especially the eucharist, should be thought of as "only symbols." The question is whether there can be any such thing. Either a thing is *really* a symbol or it is *not really* a symbol. Does the wedding ring signify the covenant that exists between this woman and this man, or doesn't it? Did Joshua's stone signify the renewed covenant or didn't it? Does the flag of this nation signify what this nation is now about, or doesn't it?

The profoundness of a symbol lies in its being just what it is. Giving or receiving a gift, sharing a meal, laying hands on a friend in love or blessing are profound things. A symbol is its own reality, and *in* its own reality it leads us into the profound mystery which it signifies. If a symbol is worth its name, it is so expressive of the familiar mystery which it signifies that it could never be called "only a symbol." If there were such a thing, why should we get angry when someone burns our country's flag? If a contractor goes to an Indian community to build houses and a totem stands in his way, why not just cut it down? The wedding rings that my wife and I wear are the same gold bands that my grandparents wore. If they were lost, and if they are "only symbols," why should we be upset at anything more than the high price of gold?

All true symbols shape our reality. When a symbol is brought forward or enacted, reality is altered for us. *All true symbols are efficacious.* In the very act of signifying a reality, they both make and change our reality.

How then are the sacraments different from other symbols? Only in the reality which they signify, not in their being symbols. The breaking of the bread signifies that we, though many, are one body in Christ. A flag does not signify this mystery. Going into the baptismal water signifies our going into Christ's death with him in order to live a new life. Giving a gift does not signify this mystery.

But at the same time, the familiar mysteries signified by displaying a flag or giving a gift are no less "mysteries" than those signified by the sacraments. Theology has faithfully maintained that the sacraments confer the grace of God through the merits of Christ, not through our own merits. But this gratuity, this givenness, also applies to the other familiar mysteries that symbols touch. The relationship between ourselves and nature, the care and friendships that exist between people, the visions that bind a nation together are also a given: such things are given by God, not created by our own efforts alone.

Christians have priorities among the great and gratuitous mysteries of life. This means that some symbols will be more precious than others, more central to the venture of living as Christians. This is precisely why seven sacraments came to be distinguished from the other symbols around us. But today our task is to reintegrate the sacraments into the larger human story. Any catechist or teacher will attest to this. The sacraments simply are not understood when they are put into a category by themselves. On the contrary, appreciation for the riches of the sacraments seems to develop only as people, young and old, are brought back into touch with the other rich symbols that surround them and efficaciously touch their lives.

chapter four

a workable definition

Sacraments are lived before they are put into categories and conceptualized. In arriving at a definition, we have to take into account not only the concepts our minds have created over the ages but also the experience we are living now. Chapters two and three talked about the categories and concepts, the insights and problems of past ages. This chapter proposes a definition of sacrament which tries to take all of this into account, namely, critical assimilation of the past together with the experience of the church today—the story that we live, along with the larger story that has surrounded us.

The first part of the definition is a summary of the cycle described at length in chapter one. It articulates the rhythm that makes life human, and it describes the basic elements that are found in every liturgical celebration. The actions and readings and prayers call us to remember our common story, not in the sense of merely recalling the past, but in the vivid sense of remembering how the story continues in ourselves. This is a remembering in the present tense; it is not just a calling to mind but a calling to heart.

The church—the Christian people and their action—holds

A SACRAMENT
is a festive action
in which Christians
assemble to celebrate
their lived experience
and to call to heart
their common story.
The action is a symbol
of God's care for us
in Christ.
Enacting the symbol
brings us closer
to one another
in the church
to the Lord
who is there
for us.

primacy in this definition. The phrase "Christians assemble" is in fact a definition of the church itself, the *ecclesia,* which is an assembly of believers. I have avoided the word "community" because it is not very accurate in this context. Documents of the early church which describe the close relationship that ought to exist among Christians speak often of *koinonia,* a Greek word which is best translated as "fellowship." Christians who assemble for worship already belong to many communities (family, social, civic, etc.). People who feel that their parish is, for them, a primary community are but one community among others in the parish. The community that celebrates the sacraments is normally an assembly of many communities; and in the act of celebrating, the assembly is called to become a fellowship.

(Sometimes it even happens to folks in the Community of the Five Rear Pews.)

The phrase "to celebrate their lived experience" can be a bit troublesome. Most Catholics grew up with the idea that the sacraments are good things, to be received as often as possible. How good a Catholic you were was often measured by how frequently you went to the sacraments. A sacrament will "take" like a vaccination, just so long as there are no antibodies like mortal sin. I intend no disrespect here. That gross image is perfectly parallel to the idea of Duns Scotus, endorsed by the Council of Trent, that sacraments will have an effect provided that no obstacle is put in their way. A minimal disposition is all that is needed. During the centuries after Trent, theologians spilled much ink in defining just what constitutes a minimal disposition.

At its core, this theology was trying to preserve a basic sacramental principle which we have already seen several times: The effects of a sacrament are God's work, not the result of our own efforts. But today we are concerned with other principles which are no less important. The *Constitution on the Liturgy* of Vatican II turned us in a new direction when it told us to pick up where the Council of Trent left off. If Trent reaffirmed the *fact* of the sacraments, we must also respect the sacraments precisely as signs and turn our attention to the *act* of celebrating them (#59). The grace of the sacraments is given by God, but that grace simply cannot be understood apart from the quality with which the sign is enacted.

Respect for the sign has therefore led us to raise questions which the theology of the minimal disposition was too narrow to address: How much lived experience do we need to bring to the celebration of a sacrament? Do some rites call for a greater degree of experience than others? Penance has become a Catholic *cause célèbre* here. What does absolution do for a young child who has never really sinned? By what criteria can such a sacramental act be called "valid" if there is no lived experience? Is confession for small children really a sacrament, or is it just a formative exercise?

These questions apply to adults as well. For example, parish celebrations of communal penance or communal anointing of the sick become a sacramental abuse when there has not been sufficient preparation for them. Being sick or being sinful is a raw experience which needs to become a lived experience. This calls for *reflection,* which might have to be stimulated through weeks of preaching and preparing for the sacramental act. Sacraments celebrate the love of God *experienced and related to one's own story.* If reflection on experience is absent, there is real danger that only magic is left—and communal magic is no better than individual magic.

The eucharist raises a somewhat different problem, because from the very beginning it has been the sacrament which celebrates not just special moments like illness or radical conversion, but the everyday lived experience of Christians. Both Luke and Paul suggest that the breaking of the bread took place regularly (Acts 2; 1 Cor 11), and other early documents concur. The eucharist was adopted into the rhythm of weekly life, and it quickly became the normal way of celebrating the Lord's Day. So it remained through the first five centuries. There are indications that the eucharist was sometimes celebrated during the week on special occasions or in small groups, but *weekly* celebration was the universal norm.

The practice of celebrating the eucharist *daily* did not develop until after the sixth century. This practice was linked with the increasing incidence of private Masses. During the era of the church fathers, there is no trace of bishops or presbyters celebrating the eucharist as a private devotion, apart from an assembly. But after the sixth and seventh centuries, as monks were increasingly ordained priests, it came to be the normal thing for daily Mass to be celebrated in monasteries—sometimes several Masses a day by the same priest. There was resistance to this use

of the eucharist as a private devotion. Several local synods tried
to limit the practice, and as late as the year 1100 A.D. Carthu-
sian priests were not allowed to celebrate private Mass every
day. But by that time, daily Mass had become the rule rather
than the exception.[8]

In our own day the practice of private Mass has undergone
remarkable evolution, in little more than a decade. The new
practice of concelebration has changed priests' attitudes toward
eucharistic devotion. There are problems with concelebration;
theologians today question whether verbal co-consecration (i.e.,
reciting the words of institution together) is really what "concelebration" is all about. But there is no doubt that the practice has
worked a revolution in priestly spirituality. "Catholic priests
have learned once more to pray together. No longer are religious communities of priests faced with the supreme irony of a
community prayer-life in which everything is done in common
except the one thing Christ left them as *the* sacrament of their
unity in him."[9]

For centuries the weekday Mass had been a kind of private
devotion for religious communities and for relatively small num-
bers of more fervent parishioners. "Private devotion" is not too
strong a term: Until the reforms that followed Vatican II, the
weekday Mass was largely a completely silent affair in which the
priest and each of the faithful in attendance quietly did their
own separate things. Now we have moved into a new phase,
where the eucharist is in practice less and less a private devotion. Since the practice of daily Mass historically evolved hand in
hand with the private Mass, it is not surprising that changed attitudes toward *private* celebrations are today generating questions
about the aptness of *daily* celebrations.

The question is not whether daily Mass is theologically legitimate. That point has been sufficiently argued over the ages,
and it is agreed that each and every eucharistic celebration com-
memorates the redemptive act of Christ. But like the other sac-

raments, the eucharist is a "festive action in which Christians assemble to celebrate their lived experience and to call to heart their common story." If the actual celebration lives up to this definition—and indeed to the liturgical requirements of the rite itself—the practice of daily celebration could be doing injury to the natural rhythm of life. Few festive actions, however low key, can bear daily repetition and still retain a festive character. If the eucharist is no longer a private devotion, the question is whether it is fitting to celebrate our Christian experience in this ritual form each day. A great many Catholics, both priest and lay, have come to the conclusion that it is not.

Some parishes and religious communities are trying to restore morning or evening prayer in common, the Liturgy of the Hours, as an alternative several times a week to the daily Mass. This effort is historically, liturgically, and theologically sound. Just as the practice of benediction has declined under the impetus of liturgical renewal, so we can expect to see further evolution in the Catholic practice of daily Mass.

A SACRAMENT
is a symbol of God's care for us
in Christ.
Enacting the symbol
brings us closer to one another
in the church,
to the Lord
who is there
for us.

The second part of the definition describes the effect of the sacraments, the "increase of grace" which has long been the preoccupation of sacramental theology.

Just as the church is a we, not an it; and just as the sacraments are actions, not things; so grace is a relationship, not a
quantity. "Grace" is another name for the relationship between
God and ourselves. From the Lord's side of the relationship,
one cannot speak of "more" or "less" grace: there is just total,
amazing grace. Any problem lies in our response to that love,
and so on *our* side of the relationship one can speak of a more
and a less.

Scholastic theology wanted to stress the objective efficacy of
the sacraments. God takes the initiative in loving us, and this
love is a "given" which is communicated in the sacraments. As
for the "more" or the "less" on our side of the relationship,
theologians like Aquinas developed a philosophy of the powers
of the soul to explain our response to God's love. In this view,
grace is a "quality," an ontological reality which informs the
soul or resides in it, as form to matter or act to potency. The
"more" and "less" have to do with the soul's own disposition,
its greater or lesser receptivity or response to the sacrament.
Backed up by a solid philosophy, this explanation was both thorough and cohesive. But as the scholastic tradition went into
decadence, especially in the centuries following the Council of
Trent, this theory became more and more mechanistic and
"thingy."

The same thing befell the concept of the "indelible mark"
that some sacraments were said to implant on the soul. The theology of the sacramental "character" was a medieval theory
which originally was meant to explain why certain sacraments
are not repeated: Baptism, confirmation, and holy orders need
no repetition because their effect is permanent. The theory of
the character, in other words, was a philosophical explanation
for the church's actual practice. The later scholastics did not always heed the advice of Aquinas, who insisted that the sacramental character is not some kind of mark impressed on the
soul. "The character is Christ himself," he wrote, "and the sac-

ramental characters are nothing other than shares in Christ's own priesthood."[10]

As we saw earlier, the philosophy which the medievals exploited was oriented especially to the explanation of substances and objects. Its categories for explaining *relational* realities were weak. In our own century theologians have turned to the philosophies of existentialism, which provide a better tool for understanding relationships and relational beings. Karl Rahner's work on the church and the sacraments, and Edward Schillebeeckx' approach to the sacraments as "encounters with Christ" were ground-breaking efforts in this area. In our time it is no longer possible to speak relevantly about the grace of the sacraments except in relational terms. Thus, the new Roman rites talk continually of how the sacraments effect a deeper "relationship" or greater "conformity" with Christ.

With Christ and also *with the church*. This ecclesial effect of the sacraments was important to the great scholastics, but it came to be almost totally neglected in the late middle ages. The Renaissance which began in the 1400's brought a new emphasis on the individual person. Productive in some areas, the new individualism had some significant negative effects on theology. It probably delayed the further development of a sound theology of the church, which would have benefited all the parties who were at odds during the Reformation. In any case, as the individualism of the Renaissance took hold, theologians increasingly discussed the grace of the sacraments in terms of the individual rather than the ecclesial body.

But sacraments do not happen first to the individual. St. Paul's concept of the church as the body of Christ is more than a metaphor, more than an image of how one member cooperates with another. Like the limbs of the human body, we as church share a *common existence*. "Just as a human body, though it is made up of many parts, is a single unit because all these parts, though many, make one body, *so it is with Christ*" (1 Cor 12:12).

Just as an arm or a leg is a *living* reality only in relation to the
whole body, so our life as Christians can be understood only in
relation to the *whole body* of which Christ is head. I do not possess grace in such a way that I can speak of "my" grace. I *share in*
the life of the graced *body* which is the church.

This "theology of co-existence" runs through the letters of
Paul, and the church fathers loved to elaborate on it. Because of
this co-existence, when a minister baptizes "it is really Christ
himself who baptizes." Those are Augustine's words. The *Constitution on the Liturgy* repeats the same idea when it states that "it
is Christ himself who speaks when the scriptures are read in the
church," and he is present whenever the church prays and sings
(#7).

Some eastern rites have even avoided individualistic formulas like "I baptize you" because such formulas weaken the principle of co-existence. John Chrysostom comments on the
baptismal practice of the church in Antioch: "It is not only the
priest who touches your head, it is also the hand of Christ. This
is shown by the very words of the baptizing minister. He does
not say: *I baptize you.* Rather he says: *You are baptized.* In this way
he shows that he is only the minister of grace and only offers his
hand because he has been ordained for this purpose."[11]

The individual person is therefore not a sound starting
point for understanding what happens in a sacrament. *Sacraments happen not to the individual but to the assembly of the Lord's
body.* And as something new happens to the celebrating community, it happens to me. This is why, in the definition I propose,
the grace effected by a sacrament is stated strictly in relation to
the church: "Enacting the symbol brings us closer to one another in the church."

Isn't this formulation too humanistic? Doesn't it elevate the
human and neglect the divine? The answer is that this formulation is very humanistic indeed. But the humanism in question is

the humanism of the body of Christ. This is quite a different story from secular humanism, in which man the *individual* stands at the center of things. The definition I propose is utterly traditional. Thomas Aquinas, for example, wrote that the grace of the eucharist is the unity of the church, which is nothing other than people coming "closer to one another in the church." Baptism celebrates union with Christ in his death; the eucharist celebrates fuller communion with him. But these effects are *signified*, in the sacramental action itself, by union and communion with one another in the church which is Christ. Why else should we celebrate—here and now and in this way—except to come closer to one another in the church, and in this very way to come closer to the Lord?

I trust that the word "church" will not be heard here in a narrow and purely institutional sense. Many Christians today feel that they are on the edge of the institutional church structures that exist now. Many indeed have chosen to remain on the margins of existing church structures, for a variety of conscientious reasons, but still they celebrate the sacraments with faith and fervent dedication. In the definition I propose, "church" must be understood as the gathering of Christian believers, wherever and in whatever form this is found and lived. "Where two or three meet in my name, I shall be there with them" (Mt 18:20). Vatican II proposes this text as a starting point for understanding the presence of Christ in every liturgical celebration (*Constitution on the Liturgy*, #7). All other structural or institutional considerations are secondary to this most basic of principles.

The concern has been voiced in recent years that our worship has lost a sense of mystery, a sense of the sacred. I am never sure how to interpret this. Sometimes it means that the celebration of the Sunday Mass has become sloppy, and that many parishes have not done a good job of implementing liturgical reforms. Sometimes it seems to mean simply that we have

abandoned the use of certain stimuli that used to make us attentive to the presence of God: sanctuary bells, organ music, certain kinds of chanting, certain regalia, even certain smells like
the fragrance of incense.

If the loss of mystery has to do with poor and unprepared
celebrations, the criticism is valid. As for the other stimuli just
mentioned, however powerful or useful or beautiful they may
be, none of them constitutes mystery or sacredness. The sacredness of a sacrament is not to be found in some kind of other-
worldliness, or in stimuli that are only experienced in the church
building. The real mystery is that we, though many, are one
body in Christ in this everyday world. The real mystery is that
the church assembled to celebrate *is* Christ. The real mystery is
that we are sacred, and that we are to discover sacredness
among ourselves. As for the Lord's part in all of this, he is with
us in as simple and ordinary a way as the water we drink and the
bread we eat.

A good part of the difficulty that some people experience
regarding a loss of "mystery" in our worship comes from an individualistic way of understanding the sacraments. If the purpose of the sacraments is for *me* to come closer to God and so to
deepen *my* relationship with God, then I will want worship symbols which direct my attention "upward," and any liturgical action which directs my attention "horizontally" to the body, the
assembly, will be a distraction or an annoyance. The sacraments
have been used as instruments of personal devotion, and of
course one's personal relationship with God comes into play in
every celebration. But again, the personal effect of the sacrament is not the starting point for understanding what a sacrament means. There is a place in any liturgy for moments which
direct our attention "upward." But any liturgical celebration is
in its total thrust "horizontal." It is an expression of this body
which has come together to celebrate, in just this way, because
these folks know that they *are* one body in Christ. In this context,

the personal devotion of any individual cannot be the norm for sacramental practice.

Everything I have been saying about the theology of co-existence and its implications for sacramental practice is very precisely summarized in one norm stated in the *Constitution on the Liturgy:* "It must be emphasized that rites which are meant to be celebrated in common, with the faithful present and actively participating, should as far as possible be celebrated in that way rather than by an individual and quasi-privately. This applies with special force to the celebration of the Mass . . . and to the administration of the sacraments" (#27).

This norm leaves room for any sacramental celebration where only literally *two* Christians are present, such as an individual confession, an anointing of a sick person which involves only that person and the minister, and a Mass with a server. (Canon law requires that even a "private" Mass have at least one person assisting—hence the expression "quasi-private.")

There are pastoral needs, indeed sacramental needs, that can be healthfully met by a one-to-one encounter between a Christian and a minister of the church who acts in the church's name. The question is not whether the sacraments have an effect on individual persons. Of course they do. But our individual lives and the "increase of grace" coming from the sacraments can be understood only in relation to the body of Christ to which we belong. In that body, the grace of God is shared in the way that arms and legs share the life of the whole body. You the arm and I the leg do not have a claim to grace on our own. This is the theology that underlies the sacramental norm I quoted above, in which sacraments happen first to the assembly of Christians (be it only two), not to individuals.

Teachers who deal with sacramental formation today face no bigger challenge than that of communicating a theology of our co-existence in Christ. A fearful amount of superstition has been fostered by the theological tradition of the last few centuries which defined the efficacy of the sacraments in terms of effects on individual souls. There is no antidote to magical attitudes toward the sacraments except a theology which sees the sacraments as expressions of the church, and the church as the whole Christ on its way to God. This ecclesial principle has only begun to make its way into popular piety. Unfortunately, the theology of co-existence in Christ is not easy to communicate in a cultural atmosphere where people's first question about any venture tends to be "What's in it for me?"

"Enacting the symbol brings us closer to one another in the church, and to the Lord who is there for us." The Lord is present to us in the church and in the festive actions of us who are the church. But in the final phrase of the definition, I also want to echo the whole Hebrew and Christian vision of a God who is intimate to us, Yahweh who is there for us, long before we even think of celebrating his love and care in festive forms. Too often we have spoken of the Lord's presence in the sacraments as though he were absent elsewhere. The final phrase of the definition tries to overcome this. I mean it to suggest that the Lord is there for us both inside and outside the sacraments. The phrase is meant to be poetic and evocative. No one has ever succeeded in *defining* just what it means to come closer to a friend, much less to God. This closeness is a reality that we touch upon in lived experience and express in our stories. Such closeness cannot be abstracted into a definition.

How many sacraments are there?

Such a question is hard to handle because it deals more with arithmetic than with lived realities. Medieval schoolmen filtered out seven rites which fit their definition of sacrament, and the enumeration went hand in hand with the evolving definition. Underneath all of this was the church's actual experience at that time. On the basis of the church's *practice* throughout the eastern hemisphere during the middle ages, it was agreed that seven rites should be seen as privileged expressions of the covenant between Christ and his church.

Today we can no longer enumerate the sacraments in the same way without adding countless qualifications. Unlike the middle ages, and since Vatican II, we have separate rites for the baptism of infants and for the baptism of adults. We have a rite for confirmation celebrated integrally with baptism, and another rite for confirmation as a separate ceremony. We have several rites for penance, depending on whether the sacrament involves individual confession or communal celebration.

The schoolmen debated whether Jesus "directly" or "indirectly" instituted the rites known to their age. The Protestants who came after them tended to reject any rite that was not documented by a specific command of Christ in the gospels. This is not where the question rests today. There is no doubt that baptism and the eucharist, the "biblical" sacraments, hold a primacy today as they did in the earliest days of the church. But the church is Christ and Christ is the church. On the basis of our co-existence in Christ, Catholic Christianity has always allowed for other rituals which meet the needs and experience of the church. On the same basis, many Protestant communities today are trying to recover sacramental rituals that were lost in the heat of the Reformation's reaction to sacramental abuses.

The definition I propose speaks of the sacraments as "symbols of God's care for us in Christ." This takes account of all the sacramental actions which are now and have long been central to the life of the church: going into the water, breaking the bread, anointing with oil at the time of initiation or illness or ordination, and laying on hands or embracing at various moments of reconciliation or sending forth. Some of these were actions which Jesus used during his own ministry. Some developed later as symbols of the same care, the care of the Father, that Jesus expressed in all the gestures of his ministry. Hence the phrase "symbols of God's care for us in Christ," which accounts for later practices as well as those of the New Testament church.

Both history and our new rites make it evident that the seven sacraments enumerated by the middle ages are interrelated to one another and variously related to the life of the church. We can no longer simply "count" the sacraments. In our day it is more useful to think in terms of sacramental *categories:*

The Breaking—to use an ancient term for the eucharist—lies in the center of the circle because this is the festive action which is at the heart of the church's life. It is in the breaking of the bread and sharing the cup that the church, whether two or twenty or two thousand people, says Christ and says who it is as the body of Christ. The other sacraments are ranged around this central act of thanksgiving and always relate to it. The rites of initiation, baptism and confirmation, themselves culminate in admission to the table of the Lord. The sacraments of healing, namely penance and the anointing of the sick, express in the special experiences of illness or renewed conversion what is already expressed in the eucharist, which is the main sacrament of our reconciliation with God. The sacraments which celebrate initiation or healing, in other words, are particular symbols which link up with the same reality signified in the Breaking: namely, our being together in Christ's body, and our being healed and reconciled with God in that body.

In the west, most Christians celebrate initiation into the church separately from the eucharist which is the culmination of that initiation; this is for a variety of reasons which will be sketched later. We celebrate healing as a separate sacramental act because it is a distinct experience which calls for a distinct form of celebration. The sacraments of penance and the anointing of the sick spell out the healing which is already implicit in the Breaking, the sacrament of Jesus' reconciling sacrifice. But we have long rejoiced in these other symbolic actions which tell us still more, in the midst of particular lived experiences, of the healing and forgiveness that comes to us through Christ.

The sacraments of marriage and holy orders are still another special case. Some medieval theologians were not sure if or how to include them among the sacraments, and history makes it clear that they had good reason.

The letter to the Ephesians (5:32) describes the union between man and wife as a *mysterium,* a term that became virtually synonymous with *sacramentum.* It was on the basis of this text, which compared marriage to the union between Christ and the church, that marriage entered the list of seven. The text obviously refers to the marital relationship, not the ceremony of matrimony. But as things evolved in the middle ages, especially under the influence of canon law, the "sacrament" of marriage came to mean the initiatory rite of matrimony more than the abiding relationship.

Orders

A similar thing happened with holy orders. Originally the sacrament of orders referred to one's belonging to a collegial body which has a particular ministry to the church. In the middle ages, the sacrament came to be identified with the ceremony of ordination, which set a man apart and gave him the power to forgive sins and make Christ present at Mass. The ceremony was understood in terms of personal sacramental power, and no longer as initiation into a body of people who had collective responsibility for a particular ministry in and for the church.[12]

Marriage and orders are forms of ministry to the church and to the world. They are clearly not sacraments in the same sense as the Breaking. The festive actions that *initiate* a marriage or a special ministry to the body—commonly called matrimony and ordination—are in fact rites of initiation analogous to baptism. In speaking of marriage and orders as sacraments, the tradition has never firmly decided whether it has meant the initiatory ceremony or the ensuing new relationship. The term can be legitimately applied to both: sacrament is an analogous term. I have suggested "sacraments of ministry" as a category to take account of the Christian tradition here.

We should also be aware that the theology of ministry has taken a new direction in our time. Many efforts are being made to recognize ministry wherever and in whatever forms it actually exists. Thus, many communities have developed forms of celebration for commissioning eucharistic ministers, readers, musicians, parish visitors, catechists, and other kinds of service to the church and to the world. Can such rites of commissioning be considered "sacraments of ministry"? By analogy, they certainly can. The forms of ministry just mentioned are often temporary ministries, recognized by the local rather than the universal church. But this should not be our main criterion. Marriage was originally considered a sacrament because that body of two people images the union between Christ and his church. The sacrament of the ordained priesthood was originally the collegial body that served the church in a particular way. If sacraments of ministry involve membership in a *body of people* who serve in special ways, there is no reason why many forms of ministry cannot be called "sacramental," by analogy to marriage and orders.

Religious often wonder why their vows are not thought of as sacraments. The fact is that for a long time they were, again by analogy. During the middle ages, religious vows were seen in relation to baptism, indeed as a "second baptism." This concept was the basis for the practice of renouncing one's baptismal name and taking a new name at the time of religious profession. Taking vows thus implied the abandonment of one's former (and presumably very sinful) identity, and this "second baptism" was even thought to confer a full remission of personal sins. This theology has now been abandoned. Still, there is no reason why a vowed life in a religious community cannot be considered sacramental, by analogy to marriage and orders.

We might not want to extend the formal use of the term "sacrament" to all forms of ministry. Words are used on the basis of a lived tradition that has given them a certain limited denotation, not just on the basis of the full meaning that the word can bear. Still, there are many forms of ministry which involve not just an individual's generous service but also a recognizable ecclesial body of servants. Sacrament is not a closed and hardened concept. This applies in a special way to the category of sacraments of ministry, where more is "sacramental" than we have often acknowledged.

The middle ages liked to point out the fittingness of the number seven, because seven symbolizes completeness. This is a bit of theological "fat" which does not interest us very much in a lean age when we have so much difficulty getting in touch with even our most basic symbols. And yet, as analytical psychology has taught us, we think symbolically even when we do not perceive or recognize the symbols. At the end of this chapter of definition, I invite you to reflect on the number four, an ancient number for wholeness.

There are the four winds and the four points of the compass, the four corners of the earth. We divide the year into four seasons. The human body has four limbs, and we once looked at personality in terms of four humors. However sophisticated our science has become, earth and air, fire and water are still the four basic elements of everyday sense experience. The Garden of Eden had four rivers flowing around the tree of life, and the church has settled on four evangelists. The cross has four points, and lines intersect at the center, where the Crucified brings all things together in himself.

Even our image of God is not complete until a fourth has been added to the three of the trinity. The fourth person is ourselves, the body of Christ, we who are made in the image of God and who are called to manifest the life of God in this world. As Plato once put it, "three is the number pertaining to the idea; four is the number connected with the realization of the idea."[13]

I have proposed four categories of sacraments. Maybe this is not new at all. Maybe it has been this way for a long time, only we have not recognized it.

the
sacramental
process
chapter five

All of the great world religions share common features in their view of God and the human quest for God. Jew and Christian and Hindu, Muslim and Buddhist, all hold that there is a transcendent reality who is supremely true and good, loving and merciful. This being is not just "out there" or "up there" but is present to and immanent in human hearts. All hold that the way to him is through self-denial, change of heart, prayer, and love of one's neighbor. All see the goal of life and ultimate happiness as knowing and loving God and becoming one with him.

But not all religions are agreed on the nature of this world, particularly the relationship of the forces of good and evil as we experience them in this world. The first chapters of the Book of Genesis take a stand on creation which differentiates Judaism and Christianity from some other religions. In these opening stories of the Bible, we read that the world was created as a good world. Good and evil are not equal forces eternally competing with each other. Rather, the creative power of God holds a certain mastery over the power of chaos. Religion therefore does not consist in a process of denying this world or escaping from it. For Judeo-Christianity, religion involves a way of being in this world and journeying in it.

For us to be made "in the image and likeness of God" means that we share in God's creativity. We are to be creative as God is creative, and we are put here to share in God's mastery over the powers of chaos and evil. This is a bold vision. It is based on firm acceptance of the radical goodness of creation, and it involves our embracing the full impact of our incarnateness, our membership in creation.

On the basis of our lived experience, we form bottom-line attitudes about what makes for meaning, what makes sense of our experience. Some people hold that evil is more powerful than good; others are convinced that the opposite is true. Some see God as a threat, a superpower who is out to get us unless we toe the line. Others opt for a loving God, one who is there for us no matter what we have to endure. These contrasting attitudes are "bottom-line" in the sense that they are utterly fundamental, i.e., they form the foundation for a whole construction of the meaning of life.

The techniques of psychology can sometimes tell us why one person's bottom-line attitude toward life is optimistic and another's is pessimistic. Such attitudes flow out of lived experience and are expressed in our personal stories. Indeed, long before any one of us enters history, these fundamental stands toward life are storied in the larger myths that surround us and affect us from birth. But whatever their source may be, such attitudes can neither be proved nor disproved. They have to do with the truth that each person accepts as a guiding truth, a truth that makes sense of things. Such attitudes seem to be changed only by a new experience, by entry into a new story. We call such changes "conversion," and we describe the source of the change as a new "revelation."

We do not know the details of the lived experience that provoked the ancient Hebrews to see the world so differently from the way their contemporaries saw it. All we know is the story they have left us in the first books of the Bible. The story tells us that beginning with Abraham, around 1800 B.C., there was a fundamental reorientation toward the meaning of God and creation. God was no longer a terrible power, indistinct from nature and acting arbitrarily against humankind, playing with people like puppets. The world of God was not a separate world "up there," identified with the recurrent cycle of nature. Rather God was to be found in the midst of this world, in history, in our story, in our time, and in all the ambiguities of ordinary experience.[14]

Because of their new experience, the Hebrews rewrote the story of creation with a firmly optimistic note and with the exalted view of man and woman created in the image and likeness of God. The fruit of all this was the new attitude toward religion that I mentioned above: Religion is not an escape from this world. It is a way of journeying in this world and of entering ever more fully into everyday experience, where God is to be found.

But the devotees of a religion do not always adhere in an unwavering way to fundamental insights. As time passes there is always a certain slippage, the dimming of an attitude which was at one time a sharp realization. The prophets of Israel were always calling the people back to bottom-line attitudes which they had forgotten.

Christianity has had the same problem. One example is the way Christians have sometimes focused on an afterlife to the point where "getting into heaven" is the only real motive for religious practice. It is no secret that many Christians have gone to church weekly not mainly to give praise and thanks to God, but as a security measure, a duty that will guarantee a heavenly reward. The preoccupation with getting to heaven is a considerable change in focus from the message of the prophets and of

Jesus, who were always preoccupied with our relationship with God in *this* world.

If Christians have at times slipped into a heaven-oriented religion, we should also be aware that this tendency is a very ancient one. Many pre-Christian religions were heaven-oriented in the sense that they focused only on an afterlife, not on the day-to-day journey that we experience in this life. For example, in the Egyptian cult of Osiris and in the Persian cult of Mithras, devotees sought an instant mystical identification with God. Their rituals had to do with plugging into a divine energy "up there," and with purifying oneself from carnal existence and the contamination of life in this world. One had to establish connection with the deity, who was not present in any ordinary way to everyday experience. Once the connection had been made through celebration of the ritual "mysteries," one was exempt from many of the moral obligations of life in this world.

The difference between these religions and the religion of the Bible is immediately evident. Alexander Ganoczy, whose little book *Becoming Christian* should be required reading on the subject of baptism, sums up the difference in a spatial image. Biblical religion is "horizontal," looking to our life in time and history, our journey from past to present and into a future yet to be created. The ancient mystery religions were "vertical." If there was movement, it was only upward to the divinity. The only journey was the mystical voyage to the god. In the mystery religions, "people are asked to stop the course of time and flee to eternity (even though they may seek to assure themselves some kind of biological existence in the interim). The quest for immortality dominates this religious view of man; there is no room for a process to build up any temporal or relational history."[15]

If some Christians today implicitly live the vertical view of religion, in which the sacraments are a kind of insurance against the future, they are not the first Christians to do so. The Christians of Corinth had similar tendencies. Many of them may have been former adherents of the mystery religions, but in any event were influenced by them. The Corinthians, as we read about them in Paul's letters, were tempted to think that through baptism they had already been given a share in the resurrection, and so were set free from further obligations. For them, baptism was a mystical identification with Christ as with a cultic god. This identification solved the problems of this life, and it guaranteed heaven. Baptism was a sort of early retirement. One could simply withdraw from the ambiguities of this life and contemplate the risen Christ with whom one was securely identified.

It is against this background that Paul develops his "horizontal" theology of baptism. The human journey, our being incarnate and living out our incarnation, has been consecrated by Jesus, who totally embraced the human condition with all its ambiguity and *lack* of security. Baptism into Christ is not baptism into the glorified life of a cultic god. We are baptized into the *death* of Jesus, so that "as Christ was raised from the dead by the Father's glory, we too *might* live a new life" (Rom 6:3–4).

Later on, the symbolism would develop that when we emerge from the font of baptism we *are* risen with Christ. But Paul refuses to make this point in his earlier letters because of the distortions to which it led. Acceptance of the human condition and the pilgrimage of human life, the journey of the cross, was not a part of the mystery religions. This is why Paul emphasizes that baptism into Christ is initiation into a lifelong process, the process of doing what Jesus did even unto death, namely walking in newness of life and becoming ever more fully human.

Paul reminds the Corinthians how their religious forebears had, like themselves, received the appropriate sacraments. The Hebrews who escaped from Egypt were all baptized by their passage through the Red Sea. Just as the Corinthians have shared the Christian eucharist, so the Hebrews in the desert all shared the manna from heaven and drank from the spiritual rock that followed them. "But in spite of this, most of them failed to please God, and their corpses littered the desert" (1 Cor 10:5). One should feel the force of what Paul is saying. It would be like telling a congregation today that their ancestors were mostly lost souls, despite the fact that they were baptized and went to Mass every Sunday. Paul's point is that a sacrament guarantees nothing. In terms of the cycle developed in chapter one, sacraments are festive moments which celebrate the presence of God as we journey along the horizontal line of our pilgrimage into the future. They are not momentary connections with God which insure us against the future.

The cross and death of Jesus lie at the heart of Paul's sacramental theology, but we should not misunderstand his emphasis on the cross. There is an ascetical tradition which has been morbidly preoccupied with suffering. Sermons and meditations on the passion have often urged us to identify with the tortures of Jesus, to feel the scourging as if in our own bodies, to sense the thorns being pushed into our own heads, or think of each personal sin as a blow of the hammer driving the nails deeper into the flesh of Jesus.

But the primary significance of the cross is not in the nails, the thorns, the torture. For Paul, the cross is the final act in Jesus' lifelong acceptance of his own incarnateness; it is the symbol of his whole journey. And if Paul can write that "Christ died for our sins," he does not mean by "sin" simply our personal acts of revolt. Paul's vision, as Ganoczy puts it, is global rather than individualistic, "encompassing all the contradiction, brokenness and alienation characteristic of mankind on its journey. The cross, in its turn, becomes Paul's symbol for Jesus' accepting and taking responsibly the historical dialectic between good and evil."

The Christian undertakes the same responsibility, and this is the meaning of baptism into the *death* of Christ. "To be baptized in the name of the crucified Christ is to take on without reservation the risks inherent in mankind's pilgrimage. It means accepting responsibly that everything human can lead either to destruction or construction, to hate or love, to the assassination of life or to its burgeoning forth. Furthermore, it means taking on the insecurity and tension that go with living a pilgrimage."[16]

The journey of the cross is therefore the human journey, everyone's journey. Physical suffering may be part of it, but living in the image of the Crucified also involves other forms of courage. At times it is simply a matter of getting up in the morning and bearing with "time's jading, the jar of the cart," and taking responsibility for the construction and destruction which any day brings. "One can even say," writes Ganoczy, "that to exist is already to be crucified."[17] I would put one nuance on that statement: To *accept* one's existence is already to be crucified.

The story of Jesus is our own story, and as Christians we are invited to graft our own personal histories onto the mystery of Jesus. The mystery of him is no less than the mystery of being human, being incarnate, being the way we all are. The gospel offers no escape from this mystery, only an invitation to enter it as fully as Jesus did.

Theology throughout the ages has speculated on the person of Jesus, but no one has ever managed to say the last word. The reality of *any* person is bigger than our concepts, and no philosophy has ever succeeded in giving a final comprehensive definition of what the human person is. For Christians, Jesus stands at the center of history as an eternal question mark, challenging all of our suppositions about what it is to be human. Theology cannot erase the question mark. But still the mystery of Jesus can be expressed in reasonably plain language: Jesus is God's pledge to us that the whole venture of embracing life and becoming human is the way to God. Jesus *is* what we have all been called to *become.*

Even better, Jesus *became* everything that we have been called to become. He had a very particular call from the Father,

but so do you and I. Christians believe that Jesus pursued his
call with unswerving fidelity. He had special gifts—but so do you
and I. Our problem is thinking that he had special gifts which
protected him from the full impact of everyday existence, or
which somehow dispensed him from the things we have to endure. "Jesus could do all those great things, but he was God and
I'm not." This kind of thinking amounts to denying the incarnation which we claim as the center of our faith. It exempts Jesus
from the real world and puts him in an ideal world, so that ordinary folks like ourselves do not have to deal with the question of
Jesus in any serious way.

The mystery of Jesus is in fact the mystery of ourselves, and
Christianity is truly bold in its belief that God has said everything he finally wants to say to us in the life of one of our own,
who had to live out human existence in the same way that we do.
The tendency to idealize Jesus is normal enough. There is no
reason why we should not say wonderful things about the wonderful person who is Lord. But the wonder finally has to be
brought home to ourselves, because it is in ourselves that we finally experience the mystery of Jesus.

Carl Jung, who was not a theologian, expressed this in a remarkable paragraph which sums up the theology of the incarnation: "Are we to understand the 'imitation of Christ' in the sense
that we should copy his life and, if I may use the expression, ape
his stigmata; or in the deeper sense that we are to live our own
proper lives as truly as he lived his in all its implications? It is no
easy matter to live a life that is modelled on Christ's, but it is
unspeakably harder to live one's own life as truly as Christ lived
his."[18]

If this is true, one finally has to answer a blunt question: Do
you believe that the Father loved Jesus more than he loves you?
Anyone who believes this does not seem to have heard the Good
News.

Horizontal thinking is not easy to sustain. It seems that something deep within us yearns for the comfort of instant vertical connections with God, and there is no doubt that the sacraments have often been used in this way. This is why renewal has been necessary.

The church's new rites all reflect a "horizontal" theology, in which the moment of sacramental celebration is a culminating moment that comes after a certain process has been experienced and lived. No rite insists on this more clearly than the *Rite of Christian Initiation of Adults* (**RCIA**), which describes a process that can be outlined as follows:

Time of inquiry

Enrollment as a candidate for baptism

Time of formation (catechumenate)

Moment of choice (election)

Time of final preparation
with rites of blessing and healing

Integral celebration of sacraments of initiation:
baptism, confirmation, eucharist

Time of integration into the life of the
community (post-baptismal catechumenate)

I shall not give a detailed analysis of the whole initiatory process and all the steps in it. This would call for a book in itself. I shall concentrate only on the *sacramental process* that is involved here.

Many elements are new—for example, the idea of making a choice *after* an appropriate time of formation. Usually the moment of choice has been identified with signing up for a program of instruction, or with the actual reception of the sacrament. Also novel is the notion of a follow-up, that is, a period of meeting regularly and reflecting on what has happened throughout the whole sacramental process. Not many Christians have been assisted, after the celebration of *any* sacrament, in the work of more fully appropriating and owning the experience of the sacrament.

One of the major contributions of the RCIA is that it broadens the whole concept of *celebration.* There are many festive moments other than the final celebration of water baptism, confirmation, and admission to the table of the eucharist. The time of inquiry, during which candidates take their first steps toward the Christian community, culminates in a ritual of enrollment, when one is formally joined to the church. The time of formation, which might consist of months or years, culminates in the rite of election. This is a celebration of a twofold choice that has come to term: the candidate's acceptance of the Christian community, and the community's own acceptance of the candidate. The final period of preparation itself is marked by numerous rites of blessing and healing (the scrutinies, etc.) which are celebrated in the weeks preceding baptism.

This initiatory process beautifully illustrates the cycle which was laid out in chapter one. It involves various stages of reflection on experience, entry into the Christian story, and festive moments which celebrate different stages of the whole experience. In those festive moments there are other forms of celebration—indeed more appropriate forms, suited to one's stage of growth—than simply those rites which are formally called sacraments.

The "grace" of baptism, its effect on the soul, used to be defined in terms of the moment when the water was poured. According to the above model, however, the effects of the sacrament begin long before the final stage is celebrated. The RCIA states that those who have been enrolled as catechumens are already "joined to the church and are part of the household of Christ," such that one who dies during the catechumenate receives a Christian burial (#18). This immediately raises questions about the understanding of original sin that has long been prevalent, especially in the western church. For well over a millennium, the pouring of the baptismal water has been understood to "take away original sin."

What are the origins of the teaching on original sin, and what are we to make of it today?

From the very beginning, Christians understood that sacramental initiation and the waters of baptism placed them in a condition of hope over against slavery to sin. Baptism expressed a new beginning, a new relationship with God through Jesus and in the Spirit. Evil and sin, not just personal sin but the cosmic evil that surrounds us all, would not finally triumph over those who remained faithful to their baptism. Just as the creative power of God held mastery over the power of chaos in the very beginning, and just as Jesus was victorious over sin and death, so those who remained faithful to their baptismal life would finally be victorious over evil and sin. This was the hope with which the first Christians lived. The "forgiveness of sin" associated with baptism meant not merely absolution from one's personal faults, but above all a new standing in the face of the far more vast powers of cosmic sin and evil and death.

Every religion recognizes and has its own terms for the sin of the world. This sin is more than the sum of our own or our neighbors' or even our ancestors' personal sins. It is a cosmic thing, it is the mystery of evil that touches everyone who is born into this world, and it is a terribly real dimension of the ambiguous world into which we are born.

But the sin of the world is not exactly what we have come to know as "original sin." Early in the fifth century Augustine of Hippo, whose name we have already seen in connection with the sacramental story, added a new element which was destined to give a very particular shape to Christian understanding of the sin of the world. Augustine was the first to state that you and I are guilty of the sin of the world and blameworthy for it *before* we sin personally, indeed before we are conscious of sin or goodness.

Augustine became involved in a dispute with a monk named Pelagius, an influential spiritual director who seemed to be far too optimistic about our natural abilities to lift ourselves up by our own bootstraps, unaided by the grace of God. Augustine's dispute with Pelagius and his followers went on for years, and the bishop of Hippo drew on every source at his disposal to demonstrate that human nature is nothing without the grace of God. Among his arguments Augustine pointed to the tradition of infant baptism as evidence that we are born without grace. He reasoned that baptism must bring about a grace that was absent to a newborn child. Otherwise why would the church baptize infants, as it has "always" done?

It did not occur to Augustine to call into question the practice of infant baptism, and he did not have the resources to examine whether this practice was as traditional or ancient as he thought. He simply accepted the practice and then fashioned it into an argument against the Pelagians without any thought that the motives for baptizing children, wherever the practice existed, might not always have been identical with his own. Augustine also worked with a faulty translation of Romans 5:12 and was pressed to explain how all of us had sinned "in" Adam's sin. The upshot of all this was a teaching on cosmic sin with some new elements: Baptism removes a personal guilt which is inherited from Adam and transmitted through the male semen.[19]

Again, it is important to distinguish Christian awareness of the mystery of evil, the sin of the world, from the idea of *individual blameworthiness prior to any personal sin.* The notion that baptism "forgives original sin" in this particular sense is unknown to the church of the first few centuries. Tertullian (d. 220) held that the semen of the sexual union transmitted holiness, not sin.[20] And long before Tertullian, Saint Paul argued that a non-Christian spouse is made holy through union with a Christian spouse, on the grounds that the *children* of a Christian parent are *holy*, not unclean (1 Cor 7:14). Like Tertullian, Paul presupposes that the gift of God's love precedes sin, even apart from baptism.

Augustine looked at a current practice, that of infant baptism, and from it he argued to a theological theory. It is not until the ninth century that we find a writer reversing the argument, stating that there *is* original and individual guilt for the sin of the world, and *therefore* one must be baptized.[21] Perhaps the reversal is already implicit in Augustine. But Augustine would also have insisted that none of this makes sense apart from the faith of the church and such factors as the conscious faith commitment of a baby's parents. The subsequent tradition did not so insist.

The doctrine of original sin as we have inherited it developed only gradually. No one will deny the truth about the reality of evil that it affirms. We are certainly born into an ambiguous world where the force of sin impinges on us as quickly as the force of love. And we are certainly born with inner tendencies which, once they become conscious, show a propensity for selfishness as much as for self-giving. But in addition to this dimension of life which the doctrine of original sin has rightly recognized, we also need to be attentive to what it has left unsaid. Is it not an essential truth of Christianity that God is a total lover, so total that he loves us even before we know how to respond? Grace is a relationship. Our side of the relationship develops only gradually, but it is always a response to a love which is already there for us. What the traditional doctrine of original sin leaves unsaid is this: God loves us from the first moment of our conception.

We are born at once into the mystery of love and into the mystery of evil. Both love and sin surround us from the very beginning. But for nearly 1,500 years, following the school of thought that developed out of Augustine's dispute with the Pelagians, the western church has given a curious priority to the mystery of evil. Our pastoral approach to baptism has implied that we are *first* conceived and born into the mystery of *evil*, and only in baptism do we securely contact the mystery of love.

Once this idea came into play, it generated still others. The Christian imagination went on to create a no-man's land between heaven and hell called "limbo," a place for the souls of infants who had never sinned but who were nonetheless "guilty" of an original fault. Limbo was never an official doctrine of the church, but it was taught by all the great scholastics of the middle ages. It was a necessary consequence of a doctrinal stand which gave priority to the mystery of evil, and which made God's love somehow dependent upon the performance of the ritual of baptism.

Happily, in this whole view of things, common sense intervened and provided an escape clause for sincere non-Christians called "baptism of desire." But here is where the weakness of this whole theology shows up. In order to account for the sincerity and personal faith of millions of Buddhists and Jews and countless others, one surreptitiously confers on them a baptism which is no baptism at all, and which these folk do *not* in fact "desire."

The problem here is that under the influence of Augustinian teaching on original sin, baptism became the explanation for the presence of God's grace in this world. The cart was put before the horse, and it became accepted teaching that baptism is necessary for the salvation *of all*, whether they have heard the gospel or not. The famous text from John's gospel which says that "unless one is born through water and the Spirit, he cannot enter the kingdom of God" (3:5) presupposes that the Spirit has in fact managed to speak through the way Christians have preached and lived the message of Jesus. The all too obvious flaws and failures of Christians were never an integral part of the doctrine that baptism is "necessary for salvation." And yet Christian common sense held its own, in an involuted sort of way. What the doctrine of "baptism of desire" says, in the last analysis, is that it is one's personal faith in God and *not* baptism which is necessary for salvation.

When it is read against this whole background and burden of theological suppositions, the *Rite of Christian Initiation of Adults* is truly a revolutionary document. It gives first priority to the mystery of God's love for us, and it nowhere suggests that we need to be absolved from an original evil. The Second Vatican Council's *Dogmatic Constitution on the Church* (#16) made a dramatic move away from the Augustinian school of thought when it affirmed in so many words that God loves everyone who is born into this world, prior to baptism and apart from baptism. The RCIA spells out the same thing in the liturgical and sacramental realm. It restores to the church, both in theory and in practice, the concept of a sacramental process which recognizes our "horizontal" journey toward God. In this process, the ritual or sacramental moments do not make present a God who is otherwise absent. Rather they celebrate a love that is present to us long before we learn to celebrate it.

This shift in perspective is, I think, utterly fundamental to the Christian view of things. At the beginning of this chapter I spoke of the basic optimism of the Hebrew view of creation which we claim to inherit. Creation is good, and the human person is good, if for no other reason than that God has created and loved us before we were born. Catholic Christianity balked at the pessimism of the sixteenth-century reformers who taught that we are radically depraved, and that Christ finally does no more than cover over our radical sinfulness. But at the same time Catholicism has based its baptismal practice on the same pessimism which grew out of Augustinian thought and which generated Reformation teachings on the depraved state of human nature.

Once again, the question is not whether the doctrine of original sin says something true about the mystery of evil. It certainly does. The question is whether the doctrine as it has come down to us leaves too many important things unsaid. In the last analysis, we are dealing here with the kind of bottom-line attitudes that were discussed at the beginning of this chapter. Optimism or pessimism about human nature, the priority of love or the priority of evil—such things involve fundamental stances toward reality that can neither be proved nor disproved. One can even argue which of these stances is more authentically Christian. Each Christian tradition, including the Catholic tradition, has at different times wavered between the choices. Augustine's own pastoral writings, especially the letters and sermons written when he was not engaged in hot dispute with the Pelagians, give a primacy to grace and the love of God which is often absent from his treatises on sin and predestination.[22]

If the Catholic church took a firm stand in theory against Calvin's pessimism regarding human nature, it has at the same time lived out essentially the same pessimism in its baptismal practice. It is easy enough to insist in theory, as Catholicism has, that we are born only deprived, not depraved. But in practice this has been more a verbal than a real difference. If the mystery of evil does not *really* have a priority, why have we rushed to have infants baptized, and why have we taught generations of nurses and doctors to baptize stillborn infants and even fetuses? The RCIA restores to the church the optimism of grace and the primacy of the mystery of love over that of evil. In so doing it reflects the vision contained in the ancient Hebrew stories of creation, where "God saw that it was good." It will be interesting to see if, in the decades to come, Catholics and Protestants alike will be willing to revise the presuppositions of the last fif-

teen hundred years, and return to an older theology which recognizes the presence of God's love in this world prior to and
apart from baptism. Unless this change in attitude takes place, it
is hard to see how baptism can ever become more than a vertical
connection with God.

The notion of a sacramental process has been absent from
other sacraments than baptism. In the new *Rite of Penance,* for instance, sacramental absolution is described as the "completion"
of a process of conversion (#6), an idea which is perfectly parallel to baptism-confirmation-eucharist as the "final stage" of initiation. But this has not usually been our approach to penance.
For many centuries we have been saying, "Go to confession and
get forgiveness." The new rite says, "Experience the Lord's forgiveness, then go to confession and celebrate it."
Protestants used to say of Catholics that "Catholics go to a
priest for forgiveness, while Protestants go directly to God."
This comment was known to anger some Catholics. Perhaps,
given the way confession was often used, the remark was too
close to the truth. In any case, the new rite makes it clear that
sacramental confession does not bring God's forgiveness into
being, any more than baptism brings his love into being. The
ritual sacrament of penance is unintelligible apart from the
process leading up to it, where Christians first "experience and
proclaim the mercy of God in their lives" and then "celebrate
with the priest the liturgy by which the church continually renews itself" (#11).
It is difficult for us really to believe in the parable of the
Prodigal Father. The father had never stopped loving his son
and welcomed him instantly. He wasn't even interested in the
boy's "confession." This is not the way human justice works,
and it is not generally the way we have viewed the sacrament of
penance. Catholics have tended to see confession with the mind-
set of the elder son in the parable: You are not forgiven until

you have made your speech, recited your list of sins, given some guarantees, and proven yourself worthy to join the rest of us who haven't strayed.

But once again, do we take as our starting point the mystery of God's love, or are we to remain fixated with sin and evil? The Lord's constant and faithful love for us is *the* good news. We are never *not* forgiven. The problem is our *acceptance* of the forgiveness that is always there for us. God does break into our lives in sudden ways, but even then a process of reflection is needed for us to absorb it all. The apostle Paul was knocked from his horse and blinded at the moment of his conversion, and then had to spend days in prayer and reflection before the scales fell from his eyes. Only then was he baptized (Acts 9). The *acceptance* of love or forgiveness is clearly a different matter from being loved and forgiven.

Once we see the sacramental moment as a final stage in a larger process, it is clear that the "grace of the sacrament" is intimately tied up with *consciousness,* with a growth in awareness. The sacraments do not bring about something that was absent. Sacraments proclaim and enable us to own a love that is already present to us. A sacrament celebrates the Lord's giving, certainly. But his giving begins long before the sacramental moment. What we need to focus on, within the sacramental moment, is our taking the love of God home with us, with a fresh awareness of that love.

Celebrating the sacrament brings us closer to one another in the church, and to the Lord who is there for us. That is one dimension of the "grace of the sacrament," as we saw in the last chapter. The other dimension, perhaps the most inner and intimate grace, is the new *awareness* of the love that is there for us. Such awareness is no more instantaneous for us than it was for Saint Paul. That is why most of the church's new rites lay so much stress on the process of preparation that must precede the sacramental moment.

One sacrament has been left curiously untouched by the renewal of recent years, and that is the celebration of marriage. There are no provisions for celebrating, in a Christian way and before the assembly of the church, the stages in a couple's coming together. For many centuries marriage has been viewed primarily as a contract, and the liturgy of matrimony has centered almost exclusively on the exchange of consent which constitutes the legal bond. In our time theologians have been exploring a whole other dimension of marriage which had long been neglected. For Christians, marriage is not merely a contract but a *covenant,* a spiritual relationship modeled on the covenant between God and his people, his beloved spouse. The distinction between covenant and contract has now become part of any theological discussion of marriage, and it is clear that not every matrimonial *contract* becomes a true spiritual and sacramental *covenant.*

If the process of a couple's coming together is a gradual process of growth in understanding the meaning of their union, one could conceive of celebrating this whole process in forms analogous to initiation into the Christian community. The first stage of celebration could be a ceremony of betrothal. A second stage, parallel to the rite of election or choice, might be a formal exchange of consent and legal recognition of the *contract.* This could be followed by a final period of preparation, with appropriate rites of blessing and healing. Finally, after a sufficient period of time, there would be a celebration of the sacramental *covenant.*

Much work would obviously have to be done before such a model could be realized in practice. The rite of matrimony has for so long been tied up with legal recognition of the bond that it is difficult to separate this element from celebration of the sacramental *covenant.* Moral questions also enter in. At what stage would the couple begin living together? Pre-marital sex is considered immoral, and in the present stage of discussion on such matters, pre-marital means literally pre-nuptial. If one were to celebrate marriage in stages, and if a couple were to live together after the celebration of the contract but before the final celebration of the covenant, we would have to put some nuances on our moral theology. If a marriage can be said to have begun before the final stage of celebration, i.e., the final sacramental nuptials, we need to consider a distinction between pre-*marital* and pre-*nuptial* sex.

On the whole, we as a church have been quite deaf to the lived experience of many young couples. Many sincerely Christian couples, who have already made a commitment to one another and are in no sense "sleeping around," have decided that it is important for them to live together before they can stand up before a Christian community and call that community to witness their union. This often comes from an experience of so many bad or meaningless marriages among friends and relations. The couple want to discover the sacrament and make sure there *is* a sacrament between them before they can authentically *celebrate* it.

I am not suggesting that this is the attitude of every couple who live together before the nuptials. One might not like this form of entering a marriage, and one might counsel against it because of many possible dangers. But the fact is that in our time, when the roles and mores associated with marriage are undergoing so much change—not all of it for the worse—many committed couples are living the catechumenal model and a genuine sacramental process in their developing relationship. Can we listen to what might be authentic in all of this? We certainly have to do better than condemn people on the grounds that pre-nuptial sex is wrong. Perhaps our own categories are not as right as we think.

This is a touchy problem, and I make no pretense of saying the last word on it here. The 1980 Roman Synod of Bishops urged the development of betrothal rites, to help raise couples' awareness of the Christian meaning of marriage. Enabling couples to celebrate their engagement in the presence of the assembly would be an excellent first step toward making the church more present to the sacramental process of marriage. But this will be seen as just another isolated rite, until we do much more work on helping people to understand the full sense of sacrament as a lived process.

chapter six
sacraments for children

*I*t began some two thousand years ago in an unimportant and politically insignificant country of the Middle East. The Christian religion then consisted of a small group of people, almost all of them unlettered, who believed that a dead man would soon return in glory. Some people even quit their jobs in order to be waiting and fully prepared for his imminent return.

A thousand years later, every lettered and learned person in the western world, along with kings and emperors, claimed the name Christian. Few people quit their jobs anymore in expectation of the dead man's return. On the contrary, one could not get anywhere in the business world or climb the ladder of success unless one was a Christian. Initiation into this religion provided the fullest membership in the society of the time.

Christians should always be charismatic people, but Christianity will never again be a tiny charismatic sect, believing in an obscure condemned criminal and waiting for his imminent return. Christians should always have an impact on history, but civilization will never again be identified with a Christian church which crowned emperors and gave kings a divine sanction.

The structures of the church have changed along with the shape of the church. The roles of the apostles and other leaders described in the New Testament have little resemblance to the roles of bishops and priests in the church nowadays. Today, for example, we place sacramental leadership at the center of the priestly ministry. But liturgy did not appear as a criterion for organizing the ministry until Ignatius of Antioch, in the second century. Saint Paul does not mention liturgical leadership in *any* of his lists of offices or gifts that upbuild the community. The first signs of liturgy or eucharistic presidency as a principle of hierarchical organization appear more than half a century after the death of Jesus. We simply do not know how the sacramental life of the church was organized during the first few generations.

When we address a new pastoral problem, it is tempting to look in the pages of the New Testament for some model which we can reconstruct and imitate. But which model will it be? We have learned that if there is little resemblance between the structures of the early church and those of our own day, there is also no single model in the New Testament churches themselves. Each community had its own way of organizing its life. The church documents of every age have had the habit of looking at some contemporary practice and saying "This is the will of Christ." But history shows that it is not so simple as all that. The will of Christ is in fact quite indistinguishable from the dynamic, living process by which the church has met the needs of its people in different ways at different times.

This may seem a lengthy introduction to a chapter on sacraments for children. I have recalled some of this information simply to make it clear that it is not easy to find an *ideal* norm or even one *original* model for any church practice.

Take for example the question of infant baptism. Sources from the first and second centuries give us little information on the subject. In recent years scholars have labored over the New Testament evidence and come up with conflicting conclusions.

One view, represented by Joachim Jeremias, is that New Testament Christians *did* baptize infants, and therefore we should do the same. On the other side of the debate, Kurt Aland has argued that New Testament Christians did *not* baptize infants, but we should nevertheless baptize them. Then there is Karl Barth's position: New Testament Christians did not baptize infants, and so we should not baptize them. "The only logical possibility remaining," as one scholar remarks, "is that New Testament Christians baptized infants and therefore we should *not* baptize infants. But this is rather absurd."[23]

A return to early sources is precious for reminding us that other ages have done things differently from the way we do them—in some cases better, in some cases worse. But in the matter of sacraments for children, it is evident that while we have to be in touch with sources, the practices of another age are not going to provide simple answers to our own pastoral questions. We are not the New Testament church, nor for that matter are we the nineteenth-century church.

A special circumstance for the church of today, particularly in North America, is that sacramental practices for children have long been associated with the school system and classroom models of instruction. For most people the question "At what age should children receive first communion?" means in practice "What grade should they be in?" As for confirmation, in most places in North America the celebration of this rite is no longer a big family event. As a result I suspect most Catholic parents would not advert to this sacrament at all unless they were reminded of it by the confirmation preparation program when it comes along.

Should infants be baptized? At what age should young people be confirmed? What is the right age for first confession? Such questions are truly unanswerable because they are not the *basic* questions. The present system of introducing children into the celebrative life of the church is neither very old, nor did it come about by careful design. Questions of the sort just mentioned presuppose that our present structure is written in stone. The best service I can offer in this chapter is not tips for next year's sacramental programs for children, but rather some data which will provoke serious thought on what the initiation of children is all about.

Let us first look at a time when the sacraments of initiation were celebrated integrally rather than separately. Suppose you were at an Easter Vigil celebrated somewhere around the fourth century. The Christian community is gathered in a large room, and the bishop or chief pastor is with them. Everyone is singing hymns, meditating on scripture readings, and praying for the candidates who are to be initiated that night or at dawn. It is an all-night vigil of prayer.

The people who are to be baptized are not in that room. They are out in the garden next to the fountain. Or perhaps the big house has a baptistry built onto it, a side room with a pool in it (the first church buildings were baptistries, not eucharistic halls). There are some deacons and presbyters with the candidates, and in some communities there were deaconesses.

The candidates for baptism are invited to renounce Satan, and after that they are anointed with oil by a presbyter. A deacon then goes down into the water with the person to be baptized. They walk down a few stone steps into the water and stand together in the pool. (In some places it was not considered fitting for a man to accompany a woman into the baptismal pool. Women were first ordained deaconesses more for reasons of propriety than out of considerations of equality.)

A presbyter stands beside the pool and asks the three baptismal questions: Do you believe in God the Father almighty? Do you believe in Christ Jesus, his son, who died and rose for us? Do you believe in the Holy Spirit, in the holy church? The candidate answers "I do believe" to each question. After each question the person is baptized by the deacon(ess). Then the candidate comes out of the pool and is anointed with oil a second time by the presbyter.

The newly baptized put on their new white garments, and together they enter the main room where the church is gathered. They go to the bishop, who lays his hands on them and prays that they may be worthy to be filled with the Holy Spirit. He then anoints them with the oil of thanksgiving, gives them a kiss, and welcomes them into the community. Now, for the first time, the newly baptized exchange the kiss of peace and pray together with the whole assembly. Bread and wine are brought forward and the eucharistic prayer is sung. All break bread and share the cup together. Admission to the eucharistic table is thus the culmination and conclusion of the rite of initiation.

What did the early Christians understand by this rich celebration? In the early centuries, initiation meant beginning a new life in Christ and thus leaving behind one's old or former way of living. This was the "first generation" experience, and it was obviously an adult experience. That is, it was adult experience that provided the norm for understanding the meaning of Christian initiation. The place of children or infants was *derivative*. Children were baptized, but the Christians of this era would not have thought in terms of "infant baptism." Their concept would have been more that of "family baptism," because whatever was done with children presupposed a view of the family as microchurch, the core faith community which would nourish the growth of the child.

During these early centuries, the meaning of Christian initiation was so tied up with the paschal mystery, the death and resurrection of the Lord, that it was not fitting to celebrate initiation except at the paschal season. The emphasis was on Christ's death and resurrection and on the process by which catechumens gradually entered into that event. There was no rush to baptize adults, much less children or infants.

A new phase which might be called the "second genera-tion" experience took hold as the emphasis shifted to the initia-tion of children, that is, the newly born children of those who were already Christians. The initiation of children was not in it-self a problem. The problem is the theology that happened to develop along with the second-generation experience, as initia-tion became something primarily for children. Especially under the influence of Augustine's teaching on original sin, the mean-ing of initiation changed. Augustine, as we saw, taught that indi-vidual persons are guilty of Adam's sin even prior to any personal sin. So baptism came to answer a need for forgiveness from inherited guilt.[24]

This changed the whole focus of initiation. First, it encour-aged the practice of baptizing infants as soon as possible, lest they go to hell or limbo if they should die. Second, baptism be-came more and more dissociated from any kind of inner conver-sion, even the interior renewal of family and community which alone justifies infant baptism. Finally, the link with the paschal season was lost. The celebration of baptism came to depend on when a child was born, not on when the whole church solemnly celebrated the death and resurrection of Christ.

In sum, the connection was lost between the faith of the church, concretely represented in the worshiping assembly, and the spiritual welfare of the infant. It eventually made no differ-ence where or when baptism was administered, just so long as the water was poured and the right words were said. The "faith of the church" became an abstraction which theologians wrote about and which one might hear about in sermons, but it was no longer expressed in the baptismal act.

The *Rite of Christian Initiation of Adults* runs counter to all of these developments and is, as I mentioned earlier, a revolution-ary document. It "turns us back" not to an old way of doing things (the rite is not a mere repetition of patristic practices) but to a more authentically Christian understanding of the meaning of initiation. I have already mentioned some of the main theological implications of this rite. Here we need to consider how the adult rite impacts on our practices with children.

The essential point is that the church's understanding of initiation is most fully *expressed* when an adult is initiated. Adult experience is *normative* for our understanding of what baptism is all about, and the place of children is again made *derivative,* as in the first-generation experience described above.[25] This means that when we look at sacraments for children, we must keep in mind the principles of the adult rite. I do not mean to propose a new legalism here, as if the letter of the RCIA can be used to resolve matters of pastoral practice. Even for adult initiation, the RCIA urges us on every page to adapt, adapt, adapt. But if we are to make sense of what we do with children, and if we are to avoid a multiplication of idiosyncratic practices as each local church works out its pastoral practices, we need a unified vision based on a consistent theology.

Recent changes in confirmation practices show the pressing need for a consistent theology. Various dioceses have moved confirmation from grade school to the later years of high school, on the basis that adult commitment cannot be expected of young children. The question is whether confirmation is *meant* to be a rite of *adult commitment.* Such changes might be a helpful solution to an interim problem, but they have been made with little or no attention to the understanding of the total initiation process which is articulated in the RCIA.

Since the church has offered us an integral vision of initiation, the principles of the RCIA will be kept in mind in the following pages as we turn to concrete questions regarding sacraments for children.

Turning first to the question of infant baptism, we should begin by correcting an idea that has appeared in catechisms. It is sometimes stated that baptism "makes us members of God's family." This idea is an appealing alternative to the abstraction which says that baptism confers sanctifying grace, but the idea is not too accurate. We belong to God's family from the first moment of our existence. Christian faith and baptism are a response to a call to belong *in a particular way* to the family of God. Through baptism we are initiated into the family of *Jesus,* into a community which is called to become aware of how the love of God has been made manifest in Jesus.

To be baptized is not to enter the world of grace, because the grace and love of God is already there, it is freely offered to all, and it surrounds the existence of everyone who is born into this world. But to be initiated into the family of *Jesus* is another matter. It is the acceptance of a very particular grace; it is a matter of entering into a conscious process in which the business of dying and rising becomes the pattern for one's life-style.

For an adult, baptism means beginning a new life in Christ, after a time of experiencing and storying that life in a Christian community. For an infant, baptism means beginning life in Christ, as one begins life in a graced and sinful world. The new Roman rite for infants is theologically consistent with the adult rite: it pays no attention to the idea of an inherited stain that needs to be washed away before one can enter the world of grace. (The term "original sin" lingers in one optional prayer.)

What about the element of conscious commitment, which is such an essential element in any sacrament? This is a problem only if we think of the sacrament as something that is done to a person, and done in a private way, rather than as something *we do* as a faith community. Recall the principle that was discussed earlier: Sacraments happen to the community, not just to the individual. The individual person is not the starting point for understanding the effects of the sacraments. The question which Augustine addressed, and which eventually gave us original sin as the chief motive for baptism, was essentially an individualistic question: "What happens to the unconscious baby who is baptized?'' Other church fathers (and Augustine himself, I think, in other contexts) would have put the question this way: "What are we doing, and what happens to *all of us* when we celebrate baptism around this child?"

The element of conscious commitment is not something that is provided only years later, when the child begins to respond consciously to baptism. It is already present—and the *Rite of Infant Baptism* insists that it *must* be present—in the faith of the parents and those who will surround the child with the atmosphere of Christian faith. The most traditional priority of the Christian church lies not with the rite of baptism itself, but with the faith of the church into which a person is initiated. This faith is not an abstraction, even in the case of infants. The rite itself is clearly addressed not to the baby but to the assembly, to the people who are responsible for creating the church around the child. Thus, whatever questions one might raise about the wisdom of baptizing infants, there is a *theological* problem only if we think of the sacrament as something that is "done to the baby" rather than as something we do as a community of faith.

In describing the ministries and offices associated with initiation, the RCIA first describes at great length the ministry of the *community,* because initiation "is the business of all the baptized" (#41). Only then are the individual ministries of sponsor, godparents, and clergy described. This is a challenging idea—and a very disturbing one, when we look frankly at the community's absence for many centuries from the whole experience of baptism, whether of infants or adults.

Every good pastor feels the pain of the present situation. An unknown couple comes to him and asks him to baptize their baby. He wants to say to them, "I don't know who you are, you have no relationship to this faith community that I am aware of, and everything inside me tells me to say *no* to this baptism." In the absence of any kind of community involvement in baptism, it is the pastor who is left standing alone to make the decision.

In recent years many Catholics have observed the baptism of infants at Sunday Mass. This practice has undoubtedly raised much awareness about baptism as an expression of the whole church's faith. But many people walking into that monthly Mass have also been heard to say, "Oh darn, I've caught the baptism Mass." The reaction is authentic, because most parishioners have had no involvement of any kind in the process leading to the baptism. Ritual alone can go only so far in involving the community. There has to be a larger community experience which backs up the ritual.

Parishes which have begun an adult catechumenate report that it is hard work getting the parish interested in the whole venture. This is not surprising. If our people have not been practically and realistically engaged in the initiation of *infants*, which is probably ninety-nine percent of our baptismal experience, how can we expect them to get interested in taking responsibility for the initiation of *adults?* But this suggests a practical corollary: There is probably no better starting point for interesting our people in the catechumenate than in getting them involved in the pastoral care of young couples who request baptism for their newborn children.

Many young Catholics drop out of close parish involvement when they leave grade school. During the high school years, religious activities are generally associated with the Catholic school or other youth groups rather than with the parish. As for early adulthood, few parishes are attentive to the situation of young singles. The parish again picks up young adults after they are married, especially when their children are ready to begin school. This leaves a period of some ten or fifteen years when the average parish is little present to people's lives.

The final stage of adult initiation is the "post-baptismal catechumenate," a period during which the newly baptized are more fully integrated into the life of the community. But let us not overlook those who were baptized as infants. What does the average parish have to offer to people between the ages of, say, fifteen and thirty? Is there in fact, in most of our parishes, any kind of community with which these young people can identify?

The baptism of a couple's first children often takes place during a time when the couple has only a nominal relationship to a parish community. An "Instruction on Infant Baptism" issued by the Vatican in 1980 points out that much more pastoral effort is needed in creating an effective community of faith around the child. The document talks at length about dialogue between pastor and parents, and about the assurances which must be given that the gift granted in baptism will grow through authentic Christian formation. The larger community also has an important role to play, and it is urged that efforts be made to involve many groups within the parish community in the pastoral care of young parents.

Given so many centuries of the community's absence from infant baptism, it is evident that these recommendations cannot be implemented overnight. The community's involvement in the baptism of infants might well begin with some simple but deliberate hospitality toward young parents—gestures which would make them feel welcome, and not just part of the mass at Mass. Such hospitality is a ministry in itself. It might be undertaken by a group of adults in the parish, perhaps from the CFM or couples contacted through a renewal movement like Marriage Encounter or Cursillo. *Infant* baptism should be "the business of all the baptized" no less than *adult* baptism. Whatever formation is needed for young parents should be provided by other parents, not by the pastor alone.

Follow-up is also essential, just as it is in the case of adult initiation. Instead of everything ending with the event of the baby's baptism, there could be a gathering or two later on, when the parents would be called to reflect on the baptismal experience and perhaps take a look at their own opportunities to contribute to the life of the parish. Why not have the bishop meet the parents of all newly baptized children on the occasion of his next visit? Why not have an annual celebration, a eucharist and a social occasion, which would bring together the parents of newly baptized children?

The ministry to infants is obviously a *ministry to parents* who will create the faith of the church around the child. We have not yet put much effort or imagination into making infant baptism an ecclesial rather than a purely individual event, a real experience of church rather than a passing ritual moment.

For the Catholic child, the elements of initiation which involve conscious commitment have long been associated with three separate rites, the three C's: communion, confession, confirmation. I have arranged these in no particular order, because the order of celebrating these rites has long been arbitrary.

Among these, *confession* sticks out like the sore thumb it has become. It became part of the initiation process for children during the middle ages, long after the original integral rite of initiation had been fractured, and at a time when confirmation had fallen into disuse. (There are indications that most medieval Christians were not confirmed.) The practice of confession for small children received fresh impetus during the seventeenth century under the influence of Jansenism, which saw sin as really more real, even for children, than the love of God.

In recent decades, sound psychological objections have been made to the practice of confession for small children. The same objections are also theological, insofar as few if any young children bring enough lived experience to the sacrament. According to the *Rite of Penance,* the "most important act of the penitent" is conversion, and this is defined as a "profound change of the whole person by which one begins to consider, judge, and arrange one's life according to the holiness and love of God" (#6). It is hard to see how any pre-adolescent child can even begin to fulfill such a condition. The introduction to the new rite speaks of penance and reconciliation strictly in terms of adult experience, and no principles are suggested for applying the rite to children.

Some Vatican officials have insisted that children should continue to make their first individual confession before first communion. This regulation, which has not been universally accepted, was not accompanied by any principles for adapting the rite to children. One might argue that confession is a useful discipline for Catholic character formation. But unless one follows Scotist theology, in which the priest's absolution is automatically powerful and the acts of the penitent are secondary, it is doubtful that many children's confessions are true *sacraments*. The practice of confession for young children is one of the more painful illustrations of how the church today "finds itself caught in tension between an old sacramental consciousness that has not yet disappeared and a new sacramental consciousness that is only in early stages of gestation."[26]

Behind all this lies the basic fact that penance is not a rite of *initiation*. It is strange that one should call for a conversion, even the kind of minimal new beginning that a child might be capable of, from someone who has not yet completed the *first* beginning, i.e., who is not a communicant and who is not confirmed. This does not imply that children should not be called to an awareness of sin, forgiveness, and the mercy of God. The question is how children can best be brought into touch with the cycle of experience-story-celebration in this whole matter of sin and forgiveness. Many catechists and pastors have found it profitable to use communal penance services without individual confession. This is a very sensible alternative to first confession at an early age.

First communion has been the Catholic child's most real and memorable entrance into the sacramental life of the church. At least this has been true in the twentieth century, because of the decree of Pope Pius X on the age for first communion (*Quam sin-*

gulari, 1910). This decree revolutionized Catholic practice in our century, but the reasons behind the pope's position are not generally known. For centuries the presupposition had been that it takes much more understanding and maturity to become a communicant than to go to confession. The tribunal of confession had become, in effect, a child's first sacramental affirmation of baptism.

Prior to 1910, American Catholic children were confirmed before they took first communion (this was the original order of the rites, though fragmented and separated by years). But before they were confirmed, they should have gone to confession: this is what various American synods of bishops urged. In some German parishes, the custom developed of delaying confession until the time of first communion, which at that time came some years *after* confirmation. One canonist, writing in 1874, argued that first confession should not be linked with first communion because this results in delaying first confession for too long. The heritage of Jansenism is evident here, coupled with an ignorance of child psychology: Young children can apparently stumble into grave sin as easily as stubbing one's toe.

In 1866, the Second Plenary Council of Baltimore had already talked about the proper age of confirmation, which should not normally be given to children under *seven.* The bishops at this council struggled with the appropriate age for first communion and finally came up with this norm: somewhere between the ages of *ten* and *fourteen.* Behind all this was the assumption that children were already going to confession.

Pius X argued against the presuppositions of the nineteenth and earlier centuries. His point was simply that if a child has enough "discretion" to go to confession, that child has sufficient discretion to be a full communicant. In effect, his decree subordinated confession to communion.

Pius X had great pastoral sense in urging that children be welcomed to the Lord's table at an early age. For centuries chil-

dren had been excluded from that action which is at the center
of the church's life. But the pope's decree prescinded entirely
from the question of *confirmation,* which now came to be celebrated *after* a child's first eucharist. A century ago, a Catholic
child was confirmed at the age of seven and began communicating several years later. For most Catholics today the procedure
has been just the opposite. In recent decades we have used confirmation as a rite of exit from grade school, or from high school
(or, as someone has suggested, a rite of exit from the church). In
sum, the developments of this century have left us with a theological and liturgical anomaly unique to the Roman church: We
have full communicants whose baptism has not been "confirmed."

What sense are we to make of confirmation as a separate
rite?

In order to see what confirmation meant for many centuries
of the church's history, let us return to the integral ceremony of
initiation which I described earlier in this chapter. The ceremony contained many ritual actions: the bath, various rubbings
with oil, prayers and kissing, and finally fellowship at the Lord's
table. It was a very sensual ceremony, and its meanings were
multiple and rich. It meant beginning a new life in Christ, being
sealed with the Spirit, receiving the gifts of the Spirit, strength
for the human and spiritual journey, embodiment in the body of
Christ.

These are the meanings of the *total ceremony.* No one part of
the ceremony had a separate and distinct meaning. There were
different symbolic actions—the bath, the anointings, the laying
on of hands, the breaking of bread. But the meaning of any of
these individual actions came from the *integral ceremony.*

Confirmation, in other words, was not thought of as a distinct sacrament with a separate and distinct meaning. Today we
associate particular meanings with confirmation, such as being

sealed with the Spirit and receiving the Spirit's gifts. But these meanings are also *baptismal* meanings.

The *Rite of Christian Initiation of Adults* insists on this connection and does not attempt to give a separate meaning to the rite of confirmation. Baptism and confirmation *together* "signify the unity of the paschal mystery, the close relationship between the mission of the Son and the outpouring of the Holy Spirit, and the joint celebration of the sacraments by which the Son and the Spirit come with the Father upon those who are baptized" (#34). It is this "unity of the paschal mystery" which we have to recover. Confirmation *cannot* be given a meaning separate from baptism and from the total process of Christian initiation. This is why, when confirmation is celebrated as a separate rite, it is urged that the sponsors be the godparents, and that no new name be taken.

The integral ceremony I described earlier began to break down at the end of the era of the church fathers, around the sixth century, when some bishops began reserving to themselves the anointing after baptism. They were unable to be present for the initiation ceremonies in all of their parishes, but they wanted to keep a role in the ritual of initiation. By reserving to themselves the anointing after baptism and various prayers for the coming of the Spirit, they could "confirm" the initiation of the candidates at some later occasion.

This sounds at first like a good pastoral idea, but let us note what is starting to happen. In the scene I described earlier, who is it that "administered" the sacraments of initiation? Clearly it was the *community* that administered the rites—with deacons, presbyters, the bishop, and the assembly itself all performing their proper liturgical functions. But now the person of the chief minister, the bishop, began to become more important than the integrity of the rite celebrated by the whole assembly. This breakdown of an ecclesial sense gradually affected all of the sacraments.

Our new rites have begun to repair this breakdown. It is now the church's law that, in the case of any candidate for baptism who is of catechetical age, the priest who baptizes is also to confirm, in the same ceremony. A bishop is not to reserve confirmation to himself unless he presides at the integral ceremony of baptism, confirmation and eucharist. It is clearly the mind of the church that this integral rite is the model and the theological norm for understanding what confirmation is about.

At present, the only instance where the church sanctions the celebration of confirmation as a separate rite is in the case of those who were baptized as infants. The above regulation could easily be extended to that case. If we baptize infants, we can also confirm them as eastern-rite Christians do, because confirmation does not have a separate meaning from baptism.

This is one direction the church might take. In that case, bishops would have to find other ways to accomplish parish visitations, which are often made on the occasion of children's confirmations. Is it really a service to a diocese that a bishop should have to organize so much of his schedule around the duty of confirming children who were baptized as babies? This practice seems truly to foster the idea that we are a child-oriented church.

To do away with confirmation as a *separate rite* is liturgically and theologically sound. This course, however, would raise problems for religious education programs. Many programs depend on confirmation as a last chance for catechizing young people. I shall return to this question in a moment. We first need to see how *catechetics* became tied up with the celebration of confirmation.

Celebrating confirmation as a separate rite, which began in a few churches in central Italy, gradually became the practice of the whole western church, as Roman practice became imposed on everyone. When Thomas Aquinas came along in the thirteenth century, the historical origins of the rite had been virtually forgotten, and Aquinas was faced with the task of giving a theological explanation for the current practice. He came up with an analogy from human growth: Just as baptism is *birth* into a new life, so confirmation signifies growth and *maturity* in the Spirit.

This idea caught on and gave a theological rationale for the separate rite. Then, during the sixteenth century, a new factor entered in. The Protestant reformers were greatly disturbed by the lack of adequate instruction which typified the church of the late middle ages. They saw a need for young people who were baptized as infants to profess their faith openly before the community. This meant that good catechesis had to be provided.

In many Protestant communities, confirmation became the occasion for such instruction. Parents were called upon to send their children to catechism classes. When the children could recite their catechism to the pastor's satisfaction, they were presented for confirmation, and then they were admitted to reception of the eucharist. Note that at this time confirmation still preceded first communion and the eucharist was the final stage of initiation, as it had been in the early church.

These are the roots of today's Catholic practice, as well as the practice of other Christian churches, where confirmation serves two purposes. One is *catechetical:* to prepare young people to make their own baptismal commitment, i.e., to affirm the faith of their baptism. The other purpose is *sacramental* or *celebrative:* that is, the community celebrates with young people a deeper conformity to Christ—a coming closer to one another in the church, and to the Lord who is there for us.

Given this complex history, and given what confirmation is supposed to signify, what is the most appropriate way to celebrate it *today?* Here are some practical considerations for pastors and catechists:

(1) *Do not try to create catechesis for confirmation which separates the meaning of that sacrament from baptism.* If confirmation happens

to be *ritually* separated from baptism, it is not *sacramentally* separate. When confirmation is celebrated as a separate rite, it becomes an occasion for young people to renew their baptismal faith. It is also an occasion for the local church to witness and accept that commitment, and for adults to reaffirm their own baptismal faith. These should be primary elements highlighted in the liturgy.

(2) *Do not teach that confirmation gives some "new" gift of the Spirit which was not given in baptism.* Confirmation as a separate rite is a sacramental occasion for deepening one's relationship to the church which is Christ. This new relationship, which the ritual often calls a deeper "conformity to Christ," is the "grace" of the sacrament. But this grace, like that of any sacrament, is measured by a person's openness to a deeper relationship *with the church.* I should repeat once again that "church" should not be restricted to mean simply the usual structures of the institutional church. Many young people who have trouble identifying with the nearby parish have found alternate forms of church in various Christian youth communities. But in any case some form of real identification with a Christian community is absolutely essential if confirmation is to make any sense. This can be a troublesome point, because openness to a closer relationship with the church in *any* form is often a problem for adolescents.

(3) *Do not teach confirmation as a rite of "adult commitment" without saying the same thing, in the same breath, about baptism.* This is where we have to part company with Aquinas, who presupposed a sacramental distinction between baptism (birth into the Spirit) and confirmation (maturity in the Spirit). This was a good way to explain the practice of that age, but our new rites no longer uphold this distinction. They insist instead on the unity of the paschal mystery and the integrity of the initiation rites. *All* of the rites of initiation are an expression of commitment to the process of becoming adult Christians, or Christian adults. If

confirmation is a rite of adult commitment, so is baptism. And so, for that matter, is the eucharist. Practically speaking, children are making a commitment to become adult Christians each time they receive communion. Christian adulthood is a process celebrated in each and every sacrament, not a specific stage celebrated in just one of them.

The following suggestions reach a bit into the future and indicate some paths we might explore:

(4) *Consider restoring the traditional order of celebrating the sacraments of initiation, so that confirmation precedes admission to the eucharist.* Our present order of celebrating the initiation of children, with confirmation some years after first eucharist, is very recent and not traditional in any sense of the word. This is not to suggest that we should go back to the days when first communion was delayed until the teenage years. But while we would not want to keep children from sharing in the eucharist, we must admit the anomaly of having full communicants whose baptism has not been "confirmed." It is the eucharist, not confirmation, which most traditionally constitutes the final stage of Christian initiation. Fidelity to tradition demands, at the very least, that we take a hard and critical look at the order we have adopted in recent decades.

One way to restore the traditional order has already been mentioned. If infants can be baptized, they can also be confirmed. Such a practice would require a change in church law, so that pastors could confirm infants at the time of their baptism. At the moment, this is normally permitted only in the case of persons of catechetical age.

Another way to restore the traditional order would be to put confirmation together with first eucharist, and celebrate the two in a single ceremony. This could easily be done under present church law, with the cooperation of the bishop. If confirmation were celebrated along with first communion, or at least in the same Easter season, there would be much less difficulty in understanding it as an integral part of Christian initiation. A separate catechesis would not have to be developed.

Both of these courses do away with confirmation as a separate ceremony. Though this is liturgically and theologically sound, either course would create a catechetical problem. One could call it the problem of the "sacramental carrot." Many of our religious education programs are based on a sacrament dangled at the end, and it is reception of the sacrament which motivates attendance at the program. For centuries, we have been using confirmation as a last chance to catechize young people.

There are many facets to this problem, including far too extensive use of the classroom model in our religious education programs. In any case, elimination of confirmation as a separate ceremony some years after first eucharist would call for serious revision of our catechetical programs. The model of the catechumenate which is outlined in the RCIA could be a rich source of new ideas here.

(5) *Consider celebrating two rites: one a sacramental rite of initiation, and the other a rite of renewal or commitment for adults.* Liturgically and sacramentally, confirmation is a rite of initiation, not properly a rite of renewed commitment. At present we are using confirmation for *both* purposes, and this is a good part of the confusion.

We may very well need a rite of passage into adulthood, or a ceremony of Christian commitment, e.g., during the high school years. This ceremony could include a profession of faith, a renewal of the covenant, a laying on of hands, a commissioning and sending forth. One could even invite the bishop to preside. This might be a ceremony not just for youth but for older people who wish, at some significant moment in their lives, to reaffirm their Christian faith.

The catechetical or faith-renewal purposes which have become associated with confirmation are legitimate concerns.

They remain a pastoral need for our time. But these purposes should be kept distinct from the sacrament which is called confirmation. If we had a separate rite of the kind just described, we could more easily return confirmation to its rightful place as a sacrament of initiation. Consultation with the Episcopal Church, which has designed two distinct rites, would be valuable here.

There are many options on which the Catholic community can reflect. And behind every question to do with confirmation lies the RCIA, which reintegrates the elements of initiation and provides a vision and a model for the future. That rite only increases the pressure that teachers and pastors already feel with regard to a separate ceremony of confirmation. It is safe to say that so long as confirmation remains a ritual separated both from baptism and from first eucharist, we are working with an interim situation. But even in that situation, there are many options we have not yet seriously weighed.

There is still another option regarding sacraments for children, and that is to consider an alternative to infant baptism. A newborn child could be publicly received into the assembly, with a ritual like the signing of the senses or some other adaptation of the first rite of the catechumenate. The child's birth, in other words, could be fully and solemnly celebrated, and the child would be joined to the church, but without the pouring of water.[27] As the child grows up, the whole process of the catechumenate would take place. Then, at the time which the parents and the community consider appropriate, the sacraments of baptism, confirmation and eucharist would be celebrated integrally. The elements of such a process, with many ritual suggestions, are already outlined in chapter 5 of the RCIA, entitled "Rite of initiation for children of catechetical age."

This suggestion does not have anything to do with "believer's baptism" as practiced in some Protestant communities. Believer's baptism involves the deferral of baptism until late adolescence or early adulthood. This practice originated at the time of the Reformation, and it was an inevitable fruit of the individualistic understanding of baptism prevalent at that time: The sacrament has its effect only if the individual can make a conscious personal commitment. Baptism thus became identified with an adult conversion experience. In effect, believer's baptism is a substitute for sacramental *penance* more than it is a sacrament of *initiation;* it is associated with the confession of sins rather than with acceptance of the church's faith. As some Protestant commentators have noted, believer's baptism is often no more than deferred infant baptism, because there is no real catechumenal process which precedes it.

In the alternative to infant baptism suggested above, the final stage of initiation (baptism, confirmation, eucharist) would not be put off until adulthood or even adolescence. The celebration might best take place between the ages of seven and nine, well before a child enters the unsettling years of puberty. Pius X reaffirmed an important Catholic tradition when he urged that children begin communicating at an early age. Full participation in the eucharistic life of the church does not demand an adult commitment, much less an adult conversion experience. Children are suitable candidates for baptism and confirmation on the same grounds that they can be communicants at an early age.

The practice of baptizing children and infants goes back to the early church, but the motive behind the early practice was not the motive of a later age. There are early sources which state that baptism should not be *denied* to children or infants, but these sources must be carefully distinguished from the much later regulation that infants should be baptized as soon as possible after birth. The practice of *requiring* infant baptism is directly based not on the early church's practice of *admitting* children, i.e., not excluding them, but on a particular theology which gave us forgiveness from inherited guilt as the motive for rushing infants to the font. This theology, as we have seen, is neither the tradition of the *whole* Christian church, nor of the Roman church itself prior to North African developments in the fourth and fifth centuries.

The canon law which states that a child should be baptized within the first weeks after birth is still on the books, and it is repeated in the baptismal rite for infants (#8). But this rite does not envision a sacramental process. Given the church's understanding of the total initiation process as articulated in the RCIA, the *intent* of the canon is that the *initiation* of the child should be seen to during the first weeks after birth. Canon law will have to be revised and brought into line with the theology of the RCIA. Otherwise the Roman church will be left with a rather ludicrous sacramental schizophrenia in which water baptism is an essential *first* stage of salvation for infants, but the *final* stage of a larger process for anyone else.

It is evident that many things would have to happen before an alternative to infant baptism could be implemented. The sacramental process described above calls for a viable Christian community which would surround and support it. As things stand, we have only begun to address the question of the community's role in *any* of our initiation practices. A whole educational process would be needed, for bishops and pastors as well as for their flocks. We would have to move securely beyond the notion that the salvific effects of baptism are not present until the water is poured. Finally, a different approach to religious education would be needed, particularly if we would no longer have any sacramental "carrots" to dangle after the integral initiation at age seven or so. Much serious thought would have to be given to the shape of a post-baptismal catechumenate for children and young people.

If these are questions for the future, we should also realize that the future is already in our midst. There is no good reason to refuse infant baptism to responsible parents who request it— but not all responsible parents *are* requesting it. Parents who no longer accept the old motive for baptism, i.e., the removal of an original stain, are already raising serious objections to rushing their newborn children to the baptismal font. The more they understand about the theology of initiation, the less inclined are many parents to proceed immediately with water baptism. An alternative to infant baptism would also be helpful in cases where young couples are not sure about where they stand in regard to the practice of their faith, but request baptism "for the family's sake." The formation process following upon the enrollment of their child and the celebration of the child's birth might be far more helpful to uncertain parents than anything we are doing for them now.

Whether it be committed Catholic couples or parents who are uncertain about their relationship to the church, there are already in our midst many young Catholics who are uncomfortable with the practice of infant baptism. Teachers and pastors should let people know that there *is* an alternative, and that the alternative is much richer than simply letting the whole thing go until children are grown up.

Obviously, an extended process of initiation would call for heightened consciousness on the part of a child's family, and it would place much responsibility on the parents' shoulders. But is the responsibility any different when we baptize infants and pick up the rest of the pieces later?

chapter seven
befriending our symbols

*I*n the course of his travels, psychologist Carl Jung spent some time among the Pueblos of New Mexico. He came to know a chief of the Taos Pueblos whose name was Mountain Lake, and the two men had many talks about the differences between the white's and the native's ways of seeing things. Whenever the conversation turned to religion, Mountain Lake was unusually closemouthed. It was only as time passed and their friendship developed that the chief let his thoughts and feelings be known. It was evident, writes Jung, that this man's religious conceptions were much more than theories to him, and his eyes would often fill with tears as he approached the subject.

On one occasion, as Jung sat with Mountain Lake on the roof of a pueblo, with the bright southwestern sun rising higher and higher, the chief pointed to the sun and said, "Is not he who moves there our father? How can anyone say differently? How can there be another god? Nothing can be without the sun." His excitement, which was already perceptible, mounted still higher; he struggled for words, and exclaimed at last, "What would a man do alone in the mountains? He cannot even build his fire without him."

The Americans, said the chief, want to stamp out the Pueblo religion. When the people want to take their children from school and lead them to the site of their sacred rites in order to instruct the children in their religion, the whites make difficulties. Mountain Lake could not understand why. "What we do," he said, "we do not only for ourselves but for the Americans also. Yes, we do it for the whole world. Everyone benefits by it."

Jung observed from the man's excitement that they had approached some extremely important element of his people's religion. Jung asked the chief what he meant by saying that their religion benefited the whole world. Mountain Lake pointed to the sun and said, "We are a people who live on the roof of the world; we are the sons of Father Sun, and with our religion we daily help our father to go across the sky. We do this not only for ourselves, but for the whole world. If we were to cease practicing our religion, in ten years the sun would no longer rise. Then it would be night forever."

At this point Jung was struck with the realization of what it was that gave the Pueblo people the sense of dignity, the tranquil composure he had so often observed. They helped the preserver of all life in his daily rise and descent, and so their lives were given a profound cosmic meaning. Jung goes on to draw a contrast between the Pueblos and our own culture: "If we set against this the meaning of our own lives as it is formulated by our reason, we cannot help but see our poverty. Out of sheer envy we are obliged to smile at the Indians' naivety and to plume ourselves on our cleverness; for otherwise we would discover how impoverished and down at the heels we are. Knowledge does not enrich us; it removes us more and more from the mythic world in which we were once at home by right of birth."[28]

Undoubtedly the biggest price we have had to pay for all

the accomplishments of reason and technology has been the loss of a myth to live by. I mean "myth," of course, not in the sense of something legendary or untrue, but in the sense of a large truth which gives meaning to life. Christianity does contain such a myth. Despite all our deviations from the original insight, our religion is rooted in the ancient Hebrew view which saw creation as good, and the human person created in the image of the creator. What this means is that you and I are indispensable for the completion of God's own creation. Jung saw this as a myth of our own, parallel to that of the Pueblos, whom we need not envy if we take our own religion seriously. The human person is "the second creator of the world, who alone has given to the world its objective existence—without which, unheard, unseen, silently eating, giving birth, dying, heads nodding through hundreds of millions of years, it would have gone on in the profoundest night of non-being down to its unknown end."[29]

The misfortune is that we have exploited this noble myth to our own near ruin. We have indeed used our remarkable creative powers to the utmost, but we have used them as much to destroy as to create. This is another way of naming original sin or the sin of the world. One can attempt many explanations of why this has happened, why we have been so destructive. A key factor, I suspect, is that we have taken our creative powers and brought them to bear immeasurably more on the outer material world than on the inner world of our own personhood. Preoccupied with using our reason to control and manipulate the outer world, we have neglected another myth which lies at the very core of Christianity, namely the myth of the incarnation. This myth, rooted in the reality and meaning of Jesus, adds yet another touch, indeed a crowning touch to the concept that we are second creators. The myth of the incarnation declares that it is the venture of becoming fully human which is the *greatest* act of creation in which we can engage.

Unfortunately, Christian theologians have tended to speculate more on theories about the nature of Christ than on the impact of the truth about our incarnateness. It is always easier to deal with someone else's sacredness than with one's own. But it must also be admitted that the Christian myth is much more difficult than the Pueblo myth. The Christian myth centers not on identification with a God who journeys across the heavens, but on a God who is finally to be found nowhere else than in one's own journey.

Rituals express the myths we live by. The religious rites of the Pueblos had to do with their task of helping the sun in its daily rise and descent, a task which benefited the whole world. The modern mind reacts to this either by appreciating the significance these people saw in their lives, or by smiling at the naive magic which such a ritual implies. Catholics should not be too quick to react in this latter way. It is not long ago that one would hear of the priest's power to make God come down upon the altar and take the form of bread and wine. This attitude toward priestly authority was based on a theology which is now outmoded, but one cannot deny that it gave meaning to countless Catholic lives. The problem is that the meaning was not close enough to the real core of the Christian myth: God's presence in this world has to do first with people and with the community of the church, not first with the elements on the altar.

I have traced many ways in which the sacraments have been understood and misunderstood. The focus of the Christian tradition has fluctuated between things and actions, the objects and the people, outward sign and inward grace. Trouble has arisen especially when the outer was emphasized at the cost of the inner, the things of the sacraments at the cost of the people celebrating them. This appears to be the history of sacramental theology. But there is a deeper issue, one which I have been trying to evoke in these last pages, and that is the question of *living the symbolic life.* Whatever defects Christians have had in their understanding of the sacraments, however lofty and ennobling or lowly and superstitious their attitudes have been, it is safe to say that past ages have treasured the symbolic life more than we do today. This esteem for the symbolic life, regularly expressed in religious rituals, gave life a powerful kind of significance which is absent today.

An old-fashioned solemn high Mass, celebrated before the Blessed Sacrament exposed, with a choir singing pieces adapted from grand opera and the Knights of Columbus raising swords in the air at the consecration, is a liturgical abortion. There are some things we cannot authentically go back to. But a word-bound liturgy in which the drone of readings and prayers, one on the heels of another, is spiced occasionally by songs like "Great Things Happen When God Mixes with People" is not an uplifting alternative.

When I was a child in a Catholic grade school, there was a chart on the classroom wall with slots for each day of the month. Into each slot we would put a small paper chasuble, colored according to the color of the vestments which Father wore at Mass that morning. It was a grand thing to see the display of red and green and white and black build up each month, and to feel the sobriety of the violet during Lent and Advent, interrupted by a single pink chasuble. The calendar of the saints no longer marks time for us, and no one would want to go back to the constant repetition of the same masses for confessors, virgins, martyrs, etc. that underlay our pretty chart. But I wish our own children had something which would give an equally vivid meaning to the passage of the days and seasons.

Catholics sometimes complain that liturgical renewal has not worked out well and perhaps we should have left well enough alone. But the problem is not liturgical renewal, which was very much needed for all of the reasons detailed in this book. The problem is that revision of the liturgy has come at a time when not many white western Christians are interested in living a symbolic life.

To live a symbolic life means to be attentive to the significance of the stuff of life, sensitive to the meaning of the activities that engage us and the things that surround us. A meal which is a true meal is more than a time for ingesting food. But today it is a standard thing to hear that "we are all so busy, and the children all have their own activities, so we usually sort of eat and run." How dangerously near this is to the world of insignificance and un-creation described in the words of Jung: "unheard, unseen, silently eating, giving birth, dying." As for the things that surround us, we fill our houses with many of the signs of material progress, but one house looks so much like another. It is rare to walk into a home where one can look around and get the feeling that people with a story of their own live here.

Jung remarked that the majority of his patients were people who had lost their faith, and who as a result had no church to help them live the symbolic life.[30] Today the problem seems to have advanced a further step. We the people who are the church have lost substantial touch with the symbolic life. We are surrounded by plenty of images, supplied in profusion by TV and the media, but we have become ever less attentive to the significance of everyday things and activities, the immediate stuff of life. As a result we have few symbols—i.e., images and things that carry *meaning*—to give shape and import and dignity to the passage of our days. We may not have lost our faith, but the expressions of it have become bland and colorless. Let us face the fact that a great many Catholics are quite *content* with the kind of worship which consists in reading through a missalette. Worship which is boring by any sound liturgical standards does not seem to be objectionable to people whose lives have no color in them.

A cultural problem lies behind our loss of the symbolic sense of things. We can admire the meaning which the Pueblos found in their lives through helping the sun in its course across the heavens. Or, to come closer to home, we can look back with a certain envy to the time when Catholics could feel they were making God more present to the world by calling him down upon the altar. But we are people of the late twentieth century, affected by many intellectual developments that cannot be overlooked. We have to bring our myths, even the most precious myths that shape our lives, into contact with the world of known facts. For good or for ill, we cannot go back and see the world in just the way that an earlier age saw it. Since men have walked on the moon, it is unlikely that anyone could ever again write a song in the simple vein of "Shine on, harvest moon, for me and my gal."

The moon can still be a genuine symbol. The moon touches our psyches in many ways; there is a human reaction to the moon which makes it more than a mere planet to be explored. But our feelings about the moon are bound to be affected by its exploration. In just the same way, our religious symbols can remain truly symbolic. They can continue to hold open for us the dimension of the unknown and the mystery of God. But, given our time and location in history, we have to let go of naive and uncritical ways of seeing our symbols.

We live our symbols long before we reflect on them and understand how they work. Chapter one noted how we are surrounded by symbols and stories which are larger than our own from the day of our birth. A child participates vitally in the stories and symbolic experiences of the family, the community, and the whole culture long before the child understands anything. Moreover, symbols always carry unconscious contents. Jesus addressed God as "father" because this image expressed the intimacy of his relationship with God. When Christian writers began to speak of Mary or the church as our "mother," this image was meant to express an intimate and nurturing relationship. But these images involve ancient archetypes, and they contain unconscious elements which we all have to sort out as we grow up. The Great Mother is both nurturing and threatening; the archetypal Father is both benevolent and punishing.

Catechesis tries to clarify the Christian meaning of symbols like God as our father, Mary or the church as our mother. But as children we live those symbols in an undifferentiated way, we live both the positive and the negative elements of symbols, long before reflection begins. Differentiation of our God-images is the work of a lifetime. In our personal spiritual growth, we all have to cover the distance from a punishing God to a loving God—from the paternalistic warrior-God who killed Egyptian babies, to the loving father who ran out to embrace his wayward son.

Symbols are very complex for a reason that is very simple: Symbols are there before we know they are there. Symbols do their thing on us before we know just what is being done. As we grow toward adult consciousness, we relate to symbols in different ways. There are two fallacies that come into play at different stages of our growth: the fallacy of *concretism* and the fallacy of *reductionism.*[31]

In the concretist fallacy, symbols are identified with the reality to which they point. There is a confusion between inner meaning and outer fact, between our names for things and the things themselves. For example, Christians believe that divine revelation is a fact, that God has shown his face to us in the history of Israel, in Jesus, in ourselves. Reflecting on all these events, we have given names to God, names that we have brought from our experience of many other realities and human relationships: Father, Son, Spirit, creator, savior, advocate. In the concretist fallacy, there is no distinction between the events of the revealing experience and the symbols or doctrines which express that revelation. This fallacy is observed in the fundamentalists of every era, who identify the symbols of our own making with the reality of God. If you don't believe the way I do, you don't believe in the one true God.

I do not need to elaborate on the fallacy of concretism as it applies to the sacraments. Concretism lies at the roots of sacramental magic, because there is confusion between the symbol and the reality upon which it touches. Baptize a baby, have a Mass said, go to confession, get a couple married in the church, and something godly will automatically happen.

The fallacy of reductionism goes in the opposite direction. In this fallacy, it makes no difference whether we have symbols or not, because all symbols are only reminders of things we already know and grasp in a rational way. I have a beautiful little wooden box that a friend made for me and gave to me after we had shared a significant time together. For the reductionist, a box is a box and friendship is friendship, and we all know what boxes and friendship are. "It's only a symbol" is the reductionist's favorite phrase. This fallacy is "based on the rationalistic attitude which assumes that it can see behind symbols to their "real" meaning. This approach reduces all symbolic imagery to elementary, known factors. It operates on the assumption that no true *mystery*, no essential *unknown* transcending the ego's capacity for comprehension, exists."[32]

The Pueblo people would eventually have to bring the myth of their religion into contact with empirically established facts about the rising and setting of the sun, just as eucharistic theology has had to deal with empirical facts about bread and wine. But Mountain Lake was not naive in his inability to comprehend our reductionism. This fallacy seems to be unique to a culture like our own which has become overawed with the power and accomplishments of reason.

No doubt, modern technology is a remarkable achievement. We have observed the world with finely tuned instruments, we have formulated laws which predict how things will behave, and we have manipulated the natural world with incredible benefit to ourselves. We have been able to overcome many forms of superstition, which is the bitterest fruit of concretism. But the reductionist sees empirical knowledge as the model for all "real" knowledge. Reductionism fails to recognize that full human reasonableness consists in more than the kind of conceptual clarity which the empirical method has taught us to seek. Thus, for the reductionist, a religious doctrine or image is not a true symbol, but only a sign for something which is already known, or which *would* be fully knowable if it were translated into a modern, nonmythical language.

We all begin our lives as concretists. Children do not actively differentiate between image and reality. Little boys who play cops and robbers, spaceman and Spiderman, or little girls who play tea party with their dolls are not usually a worry to us. Concretism becomes a *fallacy* as such only later, when one would be expected to recognize certain basic differences between symbol and reality. I am reminded of a pastor friend of mine who spices his adult-education sessions with the remark, "Folks, it's time to get out of the playpen!"

Overcoming concretism does not require a higher education in the empirical sciences. The church fathers of the early Christian era had no such education, and yet few of them were concretists. Their writings, for example, were much more attentive to distinctions between the godliness of the eucharist and the reality of God than catechisms of our own century have been. In every era, people begin their growth out of concretism as soon as they begin reflecting on the difference between images themselves and the meaning they carry.

In our time, however, growing out of concretism seems almost inevitably to involve going through a reductionist phase. This is especially true for anyone who has the benefit of a higher education, which places so much stress on the accomplishments of pure reason. Under the impact of science and technology and everything that human reason has accomplished, the stories and myths and symbols of one's youth inevitably come up for grabs. Can all these things be carried seriously and rationally into true adulthood? For a certain time in our lives, the watchwords are reason, rationality, the knowable, the known. These are the terms that bolster the fallacy of reductionism. The unknown is not really real. The unknown is simply that which is not *yet* known but *will* be known someday.

During the reductionist phase, somehow the mysteries of love and evil, sin and grace, wounding and healing, caring and not caring, all fall into the category of puzzles which somebody will someday resolve. The symbols of these experiences, which religion preserves, are a remnant of a simpler time when we were less enlightened.

The history of sacramental theology can be read as a tension between these opposite poles. Augustine opened the doors to concretism when he argued from the practice of infant baptism that the sacrament must "do" something even if the child is not conscious. Augustine himself insisted that the faith of the church is an essential element for intelligibility here, but the tradition of the following centuries did not so insist. The "thingy" approach to the sacraments which developed in the early middle ages was concretist, and this fallacy reached full term in the oath which Berengar was forced to take in the eleventh century. "The bread and wine on the altar after the consecration are not only a sacramental symbol but the true body and blood of Christ, which the priest handles and breaks and which the faithful bite with their teeth."[33] The concretist confusion of symbol with reality could hardly be more eloquently expressed.

By the time of the Reformation, sacramental concretism was so rampant that any criticism of it was bound to lean toward the reductionist fallacy, or at least *sound* reductionist. Leaving aside the question of what various reformers actually taught, I think it is safe to say that Catholics have looked upon all Protestants as sacramental reductionists. Most Catholics have been taught that for Protestants the sacraments are "only symbols," the eucharist is "only a remembrance" of the last supper, etc. On the other side of the fence, in its effort to avoid such reductionism, the Catholic magisterium has often used flagrantly concretist language.

To walk the middle path between concretism and reductionism, one must be attentive to the delicate balance between inner meaning and outer reality. For the reductionist, a symbol is an empty container into which another known content is poured. For the concretist, a symbol is a full container and not an empty shell, but the deeper reality which the symbol reveals is confused with the reality of the container itself. Both are right and both are wrong. The sun and the moon, flags and wedding rings, water and bread and wine all have profound divine and human meanings—and yet they all remain just what they are. It is in its own reality, in its being just what it is, that the symbol opens the door onto a deeper reality which cannot appear in any other form.

Chapter three talked about the nature of symbols in some detail. The question we should now consider is this: What is the *attitude* we need to bring to symbols if they are to do their work of opening us to a larger world? How does one go about living a symbolic life?

Let us suppose that these pages which you are reading were to fall into the hands of intelligent beings who know nothing of what printing and writing means. Being intelligent, they know how to put stones and beams of wood together to build houses and make fences, but they have no experience of the printed word. Upon seeing these pages, they go to work and figure out all the rules that govern the external relationships of the letters, the shape of one letter in relation to another, the frequency of certain shapes, etc. They might even come up with laws and rules about the relationships among the printed shapes which would astonish a printer. But they would never work out the *meaning* which I am sharing with you through these shapes unless they came to this page with the attitude that these inky forms do in fact contain more than interesting configurations of ink.

Before it is anything at all religious, "faith" is an attitude which we bring to our perception of the world around us. Faith is the name for that attitude which determines just how much we are going to see. The intelligent beings in my example have faith that that there is a consistency in the way these printed letters are externally related to one another, but their faith does not reach to the level of meaning. It does not occur to them that these shapes communicate a level of significance which is at once related to the shapes but also beyond the shapes.

So it is with symbols. Faith is needed if symbols are to be recognized for what they are. Loss of the symbolic sense therefore involves a loss of faith. One who has lost this faith comes to the stuff of life, the activities that engage us and the things that surround us, with the attitude that there is not really much to be seen in the spots and shapes of ink.

To live a symbolic life means that we have to take the step that is beyond building houses and fences and better mousetraps. To live a symbolic life is simply to bring faith to the stuff of life, and so befriend our symbols. I will not go on to talk of the sun and the moon, stones and flags and wedding rings, or the symbols of love and friendship which might be around the house. Suffice it to say that if we rarely reflect on our experience, and if we do not know our own stories, there will be few symbols to befriend. Living the rhythm that makes life human, the cycle of experience-story-festivity, is a sure prerequisite for living the symbolic life. Indeed, that cycle *is* the symbolic life. If it is lived, one will be surrounded with significance. If it is not lived, one has lost substantial touch with the kind of significance that raises life beyond the level of interesting configurations of ink.

If one does not live a personal symbolic life, it will be hard to grasp the symbolic life that is expressed in the sacraments of the church. The sacraments are public and communal symbols which arise from the sharing of a common experience and a common story. The common-ness of the sacraments is meant to feed and enrich our personal stories. The elements of a common experience and a common story, the first two elements in the cycle, are the dimension of life that tradition has named "the faith of the church." This faith has to do not first with dogmas, with theological abstractions, with mental acts directed to other-worldly truths. The faith of the church begins with the faith that the things of this world contain a significance which is beyond the mere shape of them.

I have tried to convey this in the definition I have proposed. "Sacraments are festive actions in which Christians assemble to celebrate their lived experience and to call to heart their common story." The faith of the church begins with the conviction that the story which we live and share is God's story as well as our own. There is hope, there is a future, and the story is not finished. But there is no other-wordly story. It is all a story about God and ourselves in *this* world.

The Christian sacraments call us back to the myth of creation and the myth of the incarnation—those largest stories of all our stories which give significance to life. To put it into the crisp shape of ink, we are second creators of the world, and the greatest act of creation in which we can engage is to become fully human. But we do not savor such profound meaning just by saying it. We story it, we enact it, we feast it. And given the convictions on which our religion is based, it is not surprising that the symbolic acts which lie at the heart of the sacraments are all expressions of human intimacy: a bath, a laying on of hands, an embrace, a rubbing with oil, a meal. These actions have become symbols of the coming of God into our lives because they are actions which have to do most marvelously and delicately with our coming closer to one another. The Christian sacraments embody, they put into body language, the import and dignity of the incarnateness we share with Jesus.

But these remarkable symbols need befriending. Think, for example, of the barriers we erect against making the eucharist an experience of breaking bread and sharing the cup as Jesus did with his friends. Obviously a large assembly cannot celebrate in the same way that a smaller group can, but I am not talking about the appropriate forms of doing liturgy. I mean simply the doing of the heart of the eucharist, breaking bread and sharing the cup, which can be done in a dignified manner whether the assembly is large or small. Could it be that we protect ourselves against experiencing the full impact of the symbolic action because it is simply too threatening? Perhaps the symbol of bread broken and cup shared is too expressive of what we ought to be as *church,* namely a body of reconcilers and reconciled who can comfortably share everyday bread and drink an exhilarating cup together.

It seems to be much easier to keep the symbol at a safe distance. So we snap a wafer which is barely visible to the assembly, distribute another assortment of wafers with all the texture of poker chips, and multiply excuses for not sharing the wine. Christian theology has always maintained that the celebration of the eucharist expresses the very essence of the church. If that is so, exactly what image of the *church* are we projecting when the bread of the eucharist is flat, thin, and tasteless?

Allow me just one more paragraph on the impoverishment of our symbols. We lack experiential contact with the symbolic dimensions of going into water, coming out of water, trusting someone to plunge us into water—or if we have reflected on that experience, we hardly associate it with baptism. Confirmation began as a rubbing from head to toe with perfumed oil, and what an experience it must have been for the assembly when the newly baptized came into their midst, truly exuding the sweet fragrance of Christ. As for today, it is hard to see what human or divine significance can be read into a flick of odorless oil on the forehead.

If I am correct in asserting that the effect of the sacraments is to "bring us closer to one another in the church, and to the Lord who is there for us," then the stuff of the sacraments is meant to express *intimacy*. It is precisely this element which minimalism suppresses. We tell people what it *means* to be baptized, what it *means* to be confirmed or anointed or whatever, and we talk the symbols to death. In the absence of an experience in which the symbols carry their own significance, we lay on a load of meanings which few will remember, simply because the meanings are not an integral part of the experience.

In this sense we are truly reductionists, trying to pour content into empty shells. At the end of the day, if I could be surrounded by symbols that really speak, I would rather err on the side of concretism. Although one must eventually overcome the confusion between inner meaning and outer reality which this fallacy entails, the concretist at least begins with the richness of things and is usually open to the effects of a symbolic experience, without having at once to intellectualize it.

Many loyal Catholics keep coming to church and keep bringing larger meanings to poorly celebrated sacraments. This is itself a form of reductionism, of trying to pump meaning into a container which does not carry its own meaning. One wonders how long this can continue. There are many indications that the next generation of Catholics, the young people already in our midst, will not tolerate sacramental minimalism. If the eucharist is not really the symbolic experience Jesus meant it to be, why bother? If one has gone beyond magic, and if a baby is "safe" without baptism, what is the point of pouring water over the child's forehead? If sacraments "effect what they signify," what effect can be expected from an impoverished symbol which signifies little or nothing?

A family once told me about one of their rituals. It is difficult for them to get together during the week, what with all the activities at school and elsewhere. But every Saturday night Dad, who works most evenings, pops popcorn. One time Grandma bought him a new popper to replace the battered old kettle he used, but Dad never used the new one. No one would think of missing this ritual, because around the bowl of popcorn the whole family shares the joys and sorrows of the week.

They usually go to different Masses on Sunday. . . .

Living the symbolic life. The symbols of intimacy that spring from our human depths are our doorway into the most human and godly things about life. The church's sacraments came from those same psychic depths, and they are meant to be doorways, through fellowship, into the unknown and into the reality of the mystery that surrounds us, the love of God that bathes us. And so we have sacraments like the bath, the meal, the feel and touch and scent of fragrant oil.

But unless we befriend these symbols more warmly and let them become the intimate experiences they are meant to be, more and more people will be looking outside the church for sacraments which will better express the love of God which they *do* experience apart from any church ritual. We are talking pure theological abstractions when we insist that sacraments do good things no matter how they are celebrated. For many folks, sharing popcorn around the dining room table just might, if you will pardon the expression, give more grace.

Is it possible to revitalize our sacramental symbols in a culture so impoverished as ours? The eminent French liturgist Joseph Gelineau recently wrote, "I have only one answer: try it, and you will be surprised. It has happened to me, and it continues to happen all the time. If all we do is *talk* to people about symbol, rituals, and liturgical ceremonies, we will accomplish nothing at all."[34]

The word *faith* usually implies a belief in doctrines. In the last decade or two, we have elucidated troublesome doctrines, improved our catechesis, cleared up many meanings. We have helped many people out of the fallacy of concretism, but in the process I fear we have often made reductionists of them. Looking at the story of Catholic Christianity, not just as it appears in the world of books and ideas but as it has been lived through the centuries, I am convinced that the particular genius of Catholicism consists in this: It is celebration, not doctrine, which lies at the heart of religion. For all of the very necessary clarification of doctrine which religious education has accomplished in our time, we need to pay fresh attention to that most basic kind of faith which consists very simply in looking at things, the stuff of our own stories, and seeing that it is significant.

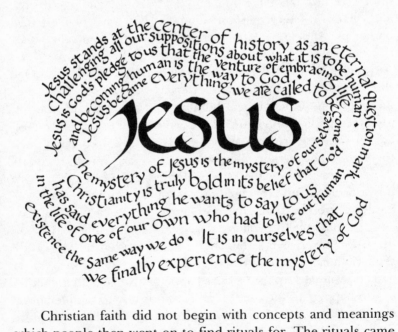

Jesus stands at the center of history as an eternal question mark • Challenging all our suppositions about what it is to be human • Jesus is God's pledge to us that the venture of embracing life and becoming human is the way to God • Jesus became everything we are called to become • The mystery of Jesus is the mystery of ourselves • Christianity is truly bold in its belief that God has said everything he wants to say to us in the life of one of our own who had to live out human existence the same way we do • It is in ourselves that we finally experience the mystery of God

Christian faith did not begin with concepts and meanings which people then went on to find rituals for. The rituals came first, because there was no better way to say it all. The disciples at Emmaus did not invent a symbol to celebrate the experience and story they had shared that day. It was in a commonplace gesture, the daily act of breaking bread, that they recognized the Lord. Try it. Take the simple and intimate things of every day, celebrate, and see if the Lord might not be there. This is the first act of faith, the first celebration of our incarnateness, and the beginning of sacramental understanding.

notes

1. "The Wreck of the Deutschland," *Poems of Gerard Manley Hopkins* (3d ed.; London: Oxford Univ. Press, 1948), p. 67.

2. Dylan Thomas, *A Child's Christmas in Wales* (London: J. M. Dent, 1968; first published in 1954 by New Directions).

3. See R. Johnston's critique of R. S. Peters and others in "The Language of Myth," *New Movements in Religious Education,* ed. N. Smart & D. Horder (London: Temple Smith, 1975), pp. 76–93.

4. C. G. Jung, "Archaic Man," *Modern Man in Search of a Soul* (first published 1933; Harvest Books edition), p. 150.

5. Harvey Cox, *The Feast of Fools* (Cambridge: Harvard Univ. Press, 1969), p. 46.

6. I trace the history of this theory in *Jesus and the Eucharist* (New York: Paulist Press, 1974), pp. 60–74.

7. *Epist.* 105.3.12 (*CSEL* 24, 604). In the historical material that follows, I shall not give detailed documentation. The material is well known and is not disputed by scholars. It can be found in any good historical survey of sacramental theology, e.g., B. Leeming, *Principles of Sacramental Theology* (London: Longmans Green, 1956).

8. On these historical developments, see the works of J. Jungmann, e.g., *The Mass* (Collegeville: Liturgical Press, 1976), pp. 63–65.

9. R. Taft, "Ex Oriente Lux? Some Reflections on Eucharistic Concelebration," *Worship* 54 (July 1980) 320.

10. *Summa theol.* III, q. 64, a. 3.

11. Chrysostom, *Second Baptismal Homily,* 26.

12. On the history of holy orders, see B. Cooke, *Ministry to Word and Sacraments* (Philadelphia: Fortress Press, 1976), pp. 574–590.

13. Quoted in J. Cirlot, *A Dictionary of Symbols* (New York: Philosophical Library, 1962), p. 256.

14. This shift in perspective is detailed in M. Eliade, *Cosmos and History* (New York: Harper & Row, 1959).

15. A. Ganoczy, *Becoming Christian: A Theology of Baptism as the Sacrament of Human History* (New York: Paulist Press, 1976), p. 27.

16. *Ibid.*, p. 39.

17. *Ibid.*

18. C. G. Jung, "Psychotherapists or Clergy," *Modern Man in Search of a Soul*, p. 236.

19. For a study of Augustine's difficulties, see G. Marvin, "Augustine's Theology and Infant Baptism," and J. Kremer, "Objective Efficacy," both in *Resonance* (1968, no. 6; St. Meinrad School of Theology), pp. 48–83. See also Ganoczy, *op. cit.*, pp. 25–68.

20. Tertullian, *De baptismo* 18.27.

21. Walafrid Strabo; see texts in *Monumenta christiana selecta*, vol. 8 (Paris: Desclee, 1959), ed. Didier, pp. 208–209, 239–241.

22. H. Rondet, *The Grace of Christ*, trans. T. Guzie (Westminster: Newman Press, 1967), pp. 89–144.

23. R. Grant, "Development of the Christian Catechumenate," in *Made, Not Born* (Univ. of Notre Dame Press, 1976), p. 33.

24. For an excellent historical summary, see D. Stevick, *Holy Baptism*, a study guide for the new Episcopalian rites (New York: Church Hymnal Corporation, 1973).

25. On the meaning of "normative," see A. Kavanagh, *The Shape of Baptism* (New York: Pueblo, 1978), pp. 102–125.

26. P. Fink, "Investigating the Sacrament of Penance," *Worship*, 54 (May 1980) 207.

27. The "Instruction on Infant Baptism" issued by the Roman Doctrinal Congregation in October 1980 states that such enrollment of infants "is not admittance to the catechumenate and the infants enrolled cannot be considered catechumens with all the prerogatives attached to being such" (#31). This is an ecclesiastical *fiat* for which no reason is given. According to this document, water baptism is an essential first step in salvation for infants, but the final stage of a larger process for everyone else. Vatican documents are usually more consistent than this.

28. C. G. Jung, *Memories, Dreams, Reflections* (New York: Random House, Vintage Books, 1961), pp. 250, 252.

29. *Ibid.*, p. 256.

30. *Ibid.*, p. 150.

31. E. Edinger, *Ego and Archetype* (Pelican, 1973), p. 111.

32. *Ibid.* Italics added.

33. Denzinger-Schönmetzer 690.

34. J. Gelineau, "The Symbols of Christian Initiation," in *Becoming a Catholic Christian* (New York: Sadlier, 1978), p. 183.

suggested readings

Bernard Cooke, *Ministry to Word and Sacraments* (Philadelphia: Fortress, 1976).

Johannes Emminghaus, *The Eucharist: Essence, Form, Celebration* (Collegeville: Liturgical Press, 1978).

Alexander Ganoczy, *Becoming Christian: A Theology of Baptism as the Sacrament of Human History* (New York: Paulist, 1976).

Joseph Gelineau, *The Liturgy Today and Tomorrow* (New York: Paulist, 1978).

Romano Guardini, *Sacred Signs* (Wilmington, Delaware: M. Glazier Inc., 1979).

Tad Guzie, *Jesus and the Eucharist* (New York: Paulist, 1974).

Tad Guzie and John McIlhon, *The Forgiveness of Sin* (Chicago: Thomas More, 1979).

Monika Hellwig, *The Eucharist and the Hunger of the World* (New York: Paulist, 1976).

Gabe Huck, *A Book of Family Prayer* (New York: Seabury, 1979).

Aidan Kavanagh, *The Shape of Baptism* (New York: Pueblo, 1978).

Raymond Kemp, *A Journey in Faith: An Experience of the Catechumenate* (New York: Sadlier, 1979).

Joseph Martos, *Door to the Sacred: A Historical Introduction to Sacraments in the Catholic Church* (New York: Doubleday, 1981).

Edward Schillebeeckx, *Ministry: Leadership in the Community of Jesus Christ* (New York: Crossroad, 1981).

Mark Searle, *Christening: The Making of Christians* (Collegeville: Liturgical Press, 1980).

R. Kevin Seasoltz, *New Liturgy, New Laws* (Collegeville: Liturgical Press, 1980).

Raymond Vaillancourt, *Toward a Renewal of Sacramental Theology* (Collegeville: Liturgical Press, 1979).

James F. White, *Introduction to Christian Worship* (Nashville: Abingdon, 1980).